The Illegals

By Tsira Gelen

Copyright 2018 Tsira Gelenava - Volobueva

License Statement

This book remains the copyrighted property of the author, and may not be redistributed to others for commercial or non-commercial purposes.

In memory of all the vanished ones who so longed to see the glorious Year of Jubilee

Chapter 1

"**W**ow!" – Exclaimed Frank. He was a no-nonsense New England Lawyer, and the look on his face told me that my brief account of our family's misadventures in the first months of our stay in America were surprising to him. "You should write a book about this." – he said.

Considering that I was still working on my historical saga at that time, the advice struck me as a daunting task, so I brushed it off skeptically:

"And who would read it? Most readers aren't interested in this."

"Why? I would. We love politics and social issues," - he protested - speaking on behalf of all Americans, of course.

"Well, we'll see." - I replied, unpersuaded.

Years have passed since that chat, and I never thought about fulfilling Frank's advice; never until now. The recent rise of heated political debates about illegal immigration changed my mind. The internet is alight with differing views, objectives and arguments.

Well, here comes my confession; although I am a foreigner and currently living in my motherland of Georgia, not so long ago I resided in the USA as an unwelcome alien for almost a decade. Not a very lucrative way to accost an already irritated reader, I guess, but do I have a choice? If I want to say anything about the matter, which I most certainly do, I have to tell the truth, the whole truth and nothing but the truth so help me God. And now, before you shove my book aside, I better start talking.

My name is Tsira which means 'young lady' in the Megrelian dialect of the Georgian language. Although I should have stopped considering myself as particularly young a long time ago, I still feel like I'm eternally trapped in that formative age. And perhaps the same linguistic magic of my funny name makes me childishly hold onto the hope that if only I find the right words, people would understand that the vast majority of illegal immigrants are just regular clean-cut, I would even say, law-abiding folks. I'm guessing that 'law-abiding' would be the key metaphor that will raise the most questions here. Of cause I'm not implying that illegality shouldn't be considered a serious misconduct. I just want to illustrate on the example that under certain circumstances even the most unlikely person might find him/herself in an unimaginable scenario.

Let's start with me.

So, what is the Law to me? In the early days of my life it had a different name – it was called "mommy's rules", and ever breaking them was absolutely out of the question. That's not because I was a good girl but because of my steadfast belief that disobeying mom was simply an impossible thing to do. Even my daddy, Nodari, a 'big' man and a 'big' boss of the 'big, big' factory, would never dare to challenge the softly spoken words of his always calm but steady as a rock wife, Madonna. Every time when I or my younger brother tried to insert his authority between us and mom's everyday requests, he would just grin and decline:

"Don't come to me. She is the queen of the house."

And indeed, she was the true ruler of our tiny private world; strict but always fair and undoubtedly always right. Of course, this innocence couldn't last forever; one day I became a teenager and the sweet taste of disobedience stealthily snuck into my heart. This is when I discovered that rules were not always so indisputable after all. But even this rebellious phase of life didn't bring the razor-sharp sensation of 'breaking the Law' into my inner world. As most of us, I went through this perilous stage of human existence quite ordinarily; not as a dazzlingly wild child but not as mommy's shy little girl either.

And then legal adulthood came, the period when all of us start seeking actual maturity and independence. That was the very first time when the definition of the word "law" truly entered my freshly developed mind, the point at which I consciously realized that I actually turned into "Tsira". Now I was totally ready to accept all of the consequences of becoming a decision maker and a master of my own life. How proud I felt just considering myself as a law abiding middle class citizen. After finishing university I married my husband Dimitri. As you see, my path through this stage of life was not extraordinary either.

The daughter of a well-off family and the wife of a hard-working and talented husband, a promising young woman myself, one of the youngest lecturers of the State University, I felt quite confident in myself and the future seemed very bright and secure. We lived in a nice apartment in a prestigious district of the capital of Georgia, Tbilisi. Our dwelling was a little bit crowded for us because we lived with my mother-in-law, sister-in-law and her son, but we were a very happy and close knit family in which all adults had well respected jobs with steady incomes and we sincerely loved each other.

And then a beautiful baby-girl entered our lives; Nino. What could be better than her? Who would even think of breaking laws in such a nirvana of complete happiness? Certainly not me. Little unavoidable lies of everyday life, harmless naughtiness here and there, insignificant mischief, well, these and other inconsequential misbehaviors, of course, sometimes took place but never true delinquency. Never an act of actual wrongdoing. I was even convinced that neither I nor any member of our family was capable of committing any serious wrongdoing.

And then boom... With the collapse of the Soviet Union the whole world collapsed around me and not only around me. One might think that finishing off a totalitarian regime and dismantling such an enormous empire is a positive thing but it's more complicated than that. Along with the liberation of many subjugated nations and granting citizens personal freedoms, which are undoubtedly great achievements, it also brought a lot of thorny, ill side effects. Unfortunately, true democracy cannot prevail on ruins of despotism right away. It requires time. Time and sacrifice of many innocent lives as old regimes almost never go without a fight. This is exactly what happened in Georgia; ethnic wars staged by the intelligence service of the former USSR, broke out and in the blink of an eye nearly a hundred percent of our relatives became homeless refugees from Abkhazia. Ethnic cleansing, bloody battles, criminal gangs all over the place, lawlessness, joblessness, and intolerable cruelty entered our lives...

That was a time when the malady of the schism plagued even the best and the most modest families. Even under such horrible consequences many tried to remain calm and obedient, always playing by the rules, but others started to seriously doubt the sanity of such inert behavior. "Fight the Devil with its own weapons," – became the most popular creed of the time, euphemistically called 'revolutionary' by historians. Many good men were broken physically and morally under such tremendous pressure; some ending in suicide, others becoming homicidal and many simply dying from heartbreak.

Our little family fought back doing everything possible to remain humane and alive. In such harsh times our second daughter, Mariam, was born - a huge surprise even for me and a real blessing to our bleeding hearts. God truly acts in mysterious ways; the more responsibility, the more reasons to stay firm and keep fighting. And so, once more we clenched our teeth and intensified our resistance to the circumstances. At that point, my husband, Dimitri, had already lost his job. The family business, a multi-profile construction complex, which we co-owned with his brother, was also under constant attack by criminals in an attempt to force us to sell it for nothing. De jure we still owned it but de facto we were not able to run it. Things were getting uglier and uglier every day but we had no right to surrender.

So, in the battle for survival, Dimitri, who was an artist by nature, noticed an abandoned basement located conveniently close to the central park of

Tbilisi. He breathed life back into that shabby little space, transforming it from a waste of space into a beautifully exotic alcove. And that is where we opened our tiny cafe. It was a desperate move, because opening even the smallest canteen without the "protection" of the local gangs was dangerous.

Consequences were swift and harsh. They came, we refused their 'protection' and they came again, but this time in masks and with guns. Of course, they took everything that they could carry. We were ruined but due to the stubbornness of our men we still didn't give up and after a while we reopened the cafe again. And they came once more. This happened three times during two months and finally we, the women, came to the conclusion that if we wouldn't halt our men, we would lose not only the goods but them as well.

That was it. After that point my husband didn't try to start another business. The only thing he was still capable of doing without any involvement of criminals was collecting fire wood in the winter and picking berries in the spring and summer. At home he entertained our kids, painting fairytale characters on our bedroom walls and playing make-believe. He would pretend to be a camel and they were princess riders on his back. This is how he kept them away from the harsh reality of our circumstances. A perfect father for our little angels.

Meanwhile, we were desperately seeking a way to create a steady income. If we failed to do so, we would parish as many others already had. As I mentioned before, our family used to be prosperous. Not very rich, but we had gained a few valuables through four generations of scholarly ancestry. So, we started selling personal belongings from our home, mainly to foreigners and sometimes to the contemporary members of our government. This decision was especially hard on my husband who already felt guilt for having failed to provide for his family. I think that the emotional damage from those days kept haunting his soul to his final days. I still remember how we would sell one tiny porcelain statuette from the renaissance era and our whole family could live for a month. Then the antique books, jewelry, a grandma's bureau, brought by her and grandpa from Paris during their honeymoon trip in the beginning of the twentieth century. Then grandpa's bronze ashtray vanished; beautiful and dear to my husband's heart.

"You never used it, anyway," - I tried to comfort him.

"Damn it and damn myself," - He grumbled back.

But those reserves eventually come to an end, and after almost half a decade of selling possessions from our home the only valuable thing still remaining there was grandma's grand piano which survived only because its sounding board, a decca, had been cracked. The last thing we sold was

Dimitri's old car. It was then when we finally acknowledged that we had no option but to sell one of us to slavery abroad. I label it as 'slavery' only from today's prospective but back then we looked at it as an opportunity to find a job. I guess many readers will not appreciate me choosing the word "slavery" to describe the situation where a person might find him/herself under these particular circumstances, but believe me, I am not using such extreme terminology in a slinky attempt to make someone feel guilty or to gain fleeting sympathy, but simply because it is the most honest way to describe a situation in which many people find themselves in due to the struggle for survival. Ironically enough, modern 'slaves' will probably hate such presentation of the truth even more than the 'slave buyers' would, but I'm abhorrent about hiding behind euphemisms.

By the way, there is nothing new or unheard of in selling oneself into slavery. It is an ancient practice which is well described in the earliest-known set of laws, the four thousand-year-old Hammurabi's code, and which, as we all witness here, successfully prevails to date. And our family was among those who dared such a fate.

Somebody told us that there was an office downtown which sent people abroad for work. So, naturally, we went to try our luck.

"For a reasonable fee, we can get a job for you in the US", - the nice lady informed us.

"How?"

"We can get a guest visa for anybody."

"Guest visa? I thought we were talking about jobs."

"Yes, but it's faster this way. We can certainly get a work visa as well, but in that case the whole procedure would take about seven years."

Seven years sounded like a hell of a lot to us. We wouldn't survive so long, but a guest visa? We still had doubts.

"Why do we need the guest visa? What can we do with it? Can we work? Is it legal?"

"Everybody who wants to work there goes through this. It's a shortcut in a formal procedure and it's absolutely legal. You go to America as a tourist, and when you're already there, you find a job and your employer goes to the Labor department and they change your guest visa into a work permit."

"As simple as that? How can we find an employer like that?"

"That's why we are here. That's our part of the deal. We already have employers. This is why we are getting paid", - was the polite answer.

"How much would all of this cost?"

"Almost nothing; $100 for a visa, + $300 as our payment, and of course an embassy fee + air tickets."

Their "almost nothing" was quite a bit of something for us but did we have a choice? No, we did not. So we started asking the details and that was when our troubles began. It appeared that in order to get a visa approval from the American Embassy we had to hide our intentions to work in America.

We didn't like it. We didn't like it at all.

"Why can't we just tell the truth? If everything you say is true, and there are jobs that Americans don't want to do themselves, then why would the Embassy deny us visas?"

"If you're so worried about a little white lie, go for it and apply for a work visa and wait seven years to get it. But first, you'll have to go to Moscow because that's the only American Embassy that does that kind of work around here."- the clerk coldly explained.

Moscow. One of the most hostile Cities for a Georgian to visit? The one where even a short stay would cost a small fortune by our standards? We couldn't afford that in a million years.

We went home completely disheartened. I'm not going to whine about all the details we had been through, recounting how difficult it was to explain to the children why we were always walking in 90 degree blistering heat when others were sitting on a bus or even taking a taxi, why mommy was always so cruel that she would only let them eat half a piece of bread at a time when they obviously wanted to munch a whole slice. I will only assure you that after we had nothing else to sell, things got much worse. The only remaining sources for survival were the little daily provisions from my parents, and kind contributions brought by our friends and distant relatives every now and again. Even refugees from Abkhazia used to help us out by sharing the monthly food donations they'd been getting from international humanitarian organizations. This is how we learned that canned meat from 1953 US Army reserves was still good. Although this was valuable knowledge about the miracles of modern food technology, it was certainly not the way of life we wanted for the rest of our lives. That was a landmark point when our bona fide principles had gotten seriously breached for the very first time. We started revising our previous thoughts and many ubiquitous doubts snuck into our hearts:

"Why do moral dogmas always get in our way?"

"Why should we follow all the rules, especially when they don't make sense?"

"Why is telling one harmless white lie so unthinkable to us?"

"A little lie never killed anyone, has it? It's our children's lives at stake, for Goodness sake! We can't jeopardize them."

That was it. We were done. We vigorously started collecting money and soon entered "the office" door once more.

"I knew you would be back", - the lady smiled. - "Don't torture yourself with fruitless doubts. This is the right thing to do. We all have been in your shoes. We all want to survive."

Before we knew it, the people from "the office" got a valid invitation from New York for my husband. We prepared all the necessary documents in accordance with their advice, sold our last valuable possessions - our wedding rings - and finally we were ready for our last and most important step; to get the visa.

"Don't worry. You almost don't have to lie", - I consoled my husband on his way to the Embassy.

He didn't answer, just looked the other way.

God, I was scared. I thought it was written on Dimitri's forehead in red marker that he was up to something and everyone was going to see it, but everything went surprisingly well that day. I was not completely dishonest while stating that he almost hadn't have to lie and "almost" was the key word there. I hadn't suspected yet that "almost" would become such a principal word in our life for many, many years. Dimitri had to leave the impression of a wealthy, flamboyant, carefree person. While this was indeed his true face in his past life, things were different now, and my husband would have to portray his old self rather than who he was now. Luckily, all of his documents were authentic. Technically, he was still a co-owner of the factory, but he had to "forget" to mention that his business had been dead for several years. But most importantly, Dimitri's affirmation that he was not planning on staying in America forever was indisputably genuine. The Embassy believed him and gave him the green light.

"You see, it was not the end of the world after all", - I comforted my husband later. – "Don't worry; the worst part of our life is over. From now we won't be starving and won't be forced to disgrace ourselves with swindling either."

If only I knew that it was just a mere harbinger of a much bigger and more colorful saga.

Getting money for the round trip ticket didn't appear hard at all. For such an occasion my father sold his car and gave us the money. I was very touched by this. I knew how much my dad loved his old GAZ 24 and what a huge sacrifice it was for him to make this decision, practically leaving his family without any source of income.

Finally, Dimitri bought the ticket.

"Be brave, woman. I'll be back in six months," – he said at last and left home, visibly trembling.

Chapter 2

It was an unfriendly, cold winter day of late December in 1997 and most of our neighbors were preoccupied with preparation for New Year's Eve. Despite the rough life and catastrophic shortage in almost everything, this time of year still remained the merriest for everybody, especially for children. I stayed in bed and silently cried all day. I didn't want to scare my girls but I was terrified. No heat, no electricity except for a few hours a day, no tap water most of the time, no money, and now no husband alongside. What should I do? How would we survive? My head was ready to explode. Thankfully, the girls, 7 and 5 at that time, didn't share my feelings at all. They hadn't even missed daddy yet, being sure that he would come in any minute.

"Mommy, aren't you going to put the Christmas tree up for us?" – They kept badgering me.

It worked, it helped me to keep my head and in a few days I was almost alright. Dimitri called as soon as he arrived in New York. We had a very brief talk, just a few comforting words and he promised me to call back straight away when he would be settled. Meanwhile the New Year came, bringing new hopes and new worries along with it. One week passed after the first call at a snail's pace but my husband didn't call back. Initially I got angry at him but then I became nervous. My friends and relatives were trying to cool me down with lame jokes.

"Who will miss a skinny one like you? He has probably already found a chubby American girl for a change", - they teased but this trick didn't overwhelm my worries.

I was getting more and more anxious with every minute and after a couple more days I went to the 'office'. It was quite chilly inside, and since the kerosene stove creaking in the corner of the room could not cope with the freezing cold, both clerks were wrapped in their coats, with scarfs around their necks. The boss was napping in a shabby armchair, and the woman was sitting at the old, slightly splayed wooden desk, devotedly veneering the peeled spots on her long nails with the bright red nail polish. The same feigned grooming, like all their business! Suddenly I got pissed off, more at myself than at the woman sitting in front of me, and hissed through clenched teeth, barely containing my anger:

"Where is my husband?"

The woman raised her head in complete ignorance. The man also woke up abruptly. An uneasy sense filled the room but pretty quickly they came round and assured me that my qualms were baseless.

"If anything had gone wrong, we would have been notified immediately. So, don't worry. We're sure your husband is fine."

Their certitude was not enough for me at all and I let them know that very clearly. The lady got annoyed at my stubbornness but still promised that she would personally find out every detail of this misunderstanding and would call me at once. And indeed, after a while she rang and told me that it had been some unexpected delay with jobs but now everything was settled. Five years earlier it would probably have been enough to cool me down but not then, not after I'd already witnessed so many betrayals and heard so many horrific stories.

"I want my husband to call me!"

"Of course; he will call you!" – The women responded irritably.

"Do something fast, lady. Otherwise I'm going to call the Georgian Consulate in New York and I will find out what's happening with my husband in my own way!" – I grumbled and hung up.

A few more days passed and during this time I had everyone in law enforcement that I personally knew or had any other way to get touch with acquainted with my troubles. All of them advised me not to jump at any conclusion yet and keep waiting. They also explained that they controlled almost everything within Georgia's borders but in order to get help in America, I had to make contact with so-called 'thieves-in-law'. Again, criminals? Even in America?! I was stunned. No way! I was not going to do such a thing under any circumstance.

After the two week nightmarish waiting Dimitri finally called. I remember that moment very clearly. I was sorting through sprouted, withered potatoes to pick out edible ones and at the same time was enthusiastically trying to assure our youngest daughter, what a wonderful dinner awaited us, if only she would wait a little longer. Poor Mariam was a mommy's good girl but still couldn't help but beg with a charming smile:

"Mom, don't feed me, just give me a little bit of bread."

I couldn't do it. We didn't have bread. I silently sobbed inside myself, but outwardly continued to cheerfully smile and kept assuring her that I would pick out the good potatoes, add the onion, a little garlic, and some melted cheese that I had hidden for such an occasion, and pretty soon the soup would be ready for the whole family. After all, good girls did not want just only them to be fed while everyone else would have remained hungry, did they? Mariam obediently nodded her head, but her huge black eyes got filled with tears. A sharp pain pierced my heart, but at that moment the phone rang and by some sixth sense I felt that it was Dimitri. I quickly wiped my dirty hands on my robe and ran to the hall. I was right. It was him. After I had learned that everything was all right with him, I started asking about the case and then I heard something very strange.

"Don't worry. I've got my passport back."

"What? Your passport?"

"Stop it, Tsira. Everything is ok. I'll call you soon."

Dimitri didn't explain anything further and simply hung up on me. Man, I was furious! Furious and immensely worried at the same time. Dimitri was a unusually strong physically and a hardy man, but he had diabetes, and he also suffered with a relatively mild form of hemophilia, but this "light form" was so insidious that for any small cuts he could bleed to death. Therefore, every time he had his tooth pulled out, he had to get stitches on the wound and had to be given special medicine to prevent bleeding. And with each such instance, I could not sleep at night, so that God forbid, some sort of trouble did not happen. Thus, you can easily imagine in what state of mind I was in.

After another two weeks of gnawing my fingernails he resurfaced again... this time from North Carolina.

"What? You disappeared and I was dying here from fear and now you're in North Carolina? What are you doing there?" – I screamed at him.

"What do you think I am doing, woman? Getting a suntan, of course!" – He shouted back.

For a few seconds I was speechless. My always calm and kind hubby had just snapped at me! It was unimaginable before. And then I heard his softened voice again:

"I work here, Tsira, mopping floors and cleaning toilets at Kmart."

Here I realized that if I wanted to learn more, I had to hold my horses and stop making his already uneasy situation even worse with my edginess. So, I pulled myself together and pretty soon I was listening to a very disturbing story. It turned out that the American business partners of the 'office' met Dimitri and a few other guys from Georgia at the JFK airport in accordance to the prearranged agreement, and then collected their passports supposedly for some formal paperwork. After that the newcomers were taken to New Ark, to some apartment where every single room was packed with people from all over the world, but mostly from the former Soviet republics, and left there without any clear explanation. I cannot tell you much about this episode of Dimitri's vicissitude because he was not talkative by nature but in one thing I can assure you: that was not the place where any human being should have belonged in. Living conditions in this temporary 'station' were awful, almost like in war stricken Georgia. For a few days Dimitri and his companions had to sleep on the floor, using their coats as blankets, in the blistering cold winter of the north-eastern coast of America. They were given very little food once or twice a day and were strictly warned not to leave the apartment, otherwise they would be arrested.

    After a couple of days Dimitri rebelled and I must tell you it was something that I would never imagine my husband would ever do as he was the most peaceful, polite, nonviolent and friendly person I've ever known. And not only did he rebel but he influenced the other Georgians to do so as well. Actually, I learned about this incident more from the secretary of the local "office" than from my husband. She shared with me behind her boss' back that the partners from New York called and complained about my husband. It turned out that on New Year' Eve Dimitri slipped out of the apartment and called his old friend who lived somewhere in Brooklyn. So, his first new year in America Dimitri spent in a serene circle of Georgian-Jewish immigrants. Apparently they had advised my restrained husband what to do in such an unusual situation. He was enlightened that since he was in the country absolutely legally, he had nothing to fear from the police, and that those guys from the office were the ones who had to worry about cops. A couple of days later, Dimitri returned to New Ark and resolutely demanded his passport back. This was a very risky step, as it was clearly smelling of organized crime, and entering into a conflict with the Russian mafia was not a joke. But God was merciful and everything worked out peacefully. They gave him his passport, but even that appeared not enough for my husband who had gone wild. I am writing these lines and I have a feeling that instead of describing the life of our most ordinary, quiet and peaceful family, I am composing some kind of crime fiction novel. But it was just like that. My most humble husband, who by the will of fate turned into the Moses for the rest of the Georgians trapped in that New Ark flat, demanded that they return the passports to all his fellow countrymen. This caused a real hassle which came down to assault, but as I noted above, Dmitri possessed incredible strength, so pressing on him physically was not so easy. Fortunately, the confrontation ended without any serious mutilation. Both sides received their fair share of cracks and bruises, but without any further complications it all ended there. As a result, all the Georgians got their passports back. That was when the business partners from New York had called the Tbilisi 'office' and demanded that they would never send them such an 'intelligent freak' ever again. Later, when I asked Dimitri what a miracle had turned my complaisant hubby into such a thug of Rambo, he replied that it was the dejection of the situation. He simply could not let them down.

But Dmitry's responsibility for those people did not end there. Being the only English-speaking person among them and having some money in his pocket, he was regarded as some kind of lifebuoy by the others, and everyone literally stuck to him. It would have been much better for Dimitri to stay in New York, where we had many friends and acquaintances, but he made a hard decision. I don't know how exactly, but Dimitri managed to contact some American woman of Bulgarian origin and explain to her their situation. It happened that she knew someone who owned a cleaning business in North Carolina and now all the Georgians from the New Ark apartment worked in a huge chain store company called Kmart.

But at the moment when I was talking to my husband on the phone, I didn't known all these details yet. So the key question that bothered me the most, after his health, of course, concerned his documents. On my inquiry if he had got a working permit, Dimitri responded briefly:

"Not yet".

"Is your employer going to do anything about it?"

His uncertain answer was: "We'll see."

Well, as you can guess, I was not completely thrilled by the fact that my delicate husband had become a public toilet cleaner but when I learned that Dimitri lost twenty-six kilograms, trembles swept through my whole being. The hidden fear that his diabetes had probably gotten worse, most likely because of the tremendous stress he had been through lately, clenched my heart in a tight fist. We knew from the very beginning that there would be no milky shores waiting for poor job seekers in America, but I could never imagine that it could be so emotionally difficult for him. I stood in the cold hallway, (we could afford to heat only the bedrooms and then only in the daytime) and nervously twisted the telephone cord in my fingers, trying not to let my voice betray the extent of my anxiety. I could not help him, but I could hurt him by displaying my weakness. So I started cheerfully saying something about Dimitri's current situation being much better than the launch of his adventures, and I thanked the Lord for the little progress we still managed to achieve and encouraged my husband by assuring him that all of the steps he had made so far were absolutely right and he should continue his efforts with the same courage.

The first month's paychecks Dimitri and his companions got had to go to the woman who had found them the jobs and they also needed some money to feed themselves too, so no help for their families had been available yet. The next two months they had to pay for a car the employer prearranged them to buy. Only in May did we receive some money from Dimitri, but it was not enough even to cover our debt for his traveling expenses. Another huge problem - at the end of June his six month visa would be expired but his employer hadn't even started the paperwork to get him a work permit. We were confused. Should he come back? He still had a return ticket. But without any money what would he do? The conditions got even worse back in Georgia. The only gleam in this stressful situation was that we regularly talked on the phone. Every day I waited for a call from America as manna from heaven. Nothing really mattered for me anymore, just to hear the voice of my beloved. I missed him terribly. At each call, I rushed to the phone like I was on fire, so that no one could beat me. If it were only for me, I would have called him back long before. But behind my back stood the whole family and I should have always remembered that. Therefore, during our brief conversations, there was almost never time for sentiments, just only deeds and deeds. Of course, the current issue was the working visa and I constantly tormented my husband with the same question:

"Why isn't your boss doing anything about your visa?"

At some point his silence gave a crack and he answered sincerely:

"You know, Tsira, it is not necessary for us to have work permits. Boss says he has to go through lots of paperwork to get them for us and he does not want to. He says personally he does not even need our work permits to keep us as employees."

Another blow to my face.

"You can't be there without a visa. They'll kick you out!"- I started arguing but he cut me short:

"No, they will not. Nobody cares about papers here."

I couldn't believe that my husband was saying that. As if my fears because of his health were not enough, now I got scared for his safety too and started begging him to get at least his guest visa extended. He took my advice, although as the future proved, he was partially right about documents and his legal papers not being important for most of the people around.

Right now it is not my intension to start speculation about this very important issue that the American legal system has stuck with for too many years, although it's extremely urgent, in my point of view, for many of its citizens. When it comes to illegality, the first thing that prompts to everybody's mind is Mexican workers and temporary agricultural jobs which they're supposedly taking from Americans. But what about others, those 2,5 million non-Mexican undocumented aliens who are left just about invisible?

In this narrative I'll tell you about one very private case of how ordinary newcomers from Eastern Europe, under certain circumstances became illegal aliens.

Dimitri and his co-workers lived together. They had only one car, so my husband used to drive all of them to their work places and only then would he go to his own. They all worked very hard, seven days a week, every single night, without any weekends; no Independence Day, no Christmas, no Easter, no Veterans Day, nor any other holiday was ever available for them, but despite such intensive labor they still had very little earnings, so little that Dimitri barely was able to send a few hundred bucks home in almost a year.

As for life in Georgia, it didn't improve a bit. Time was passing by swiftly and very soon another six month visa would be expired but we hadn't achieved anything yet; no money, no husband around. I started complaining and demanded that Dimitri should return home but my mother-in-law strongly opposed this.

The goldish weather of late autumn, so typical for Tbilisi at this time of the year, was glowing outside. The entire enclave of the inter-mountain area where the capital of Georgia is situated was literally flooded with sunlight, but it was a deceptive radiance. In fact it was quite chilly outside. Therefore, all the windows were tightly closed, but the sun's rays through the panoramic pane perfectly heated the inner space of our living room. Since these were the hours when we were given electricity, Marina, my sister-in-law, was ironing her clothes in the far corner of the room. Next to the window, her mom, madam Natela, Panica, as we lovingly called her due to her constant readiness to panic for any trifle, was resting, reclined on her couch, as usual, nervously shaking her little elegant leg, a clear sign that she was in a skirmishing mood. In such moments Marina and I always tried to dodge the confrontation with our plump snow-white. Don't get me wrong. We all sincerely loved her, but that did not mean that her sometimes intrusively provocative character didn't test our self-control, which, I must admit, every now and then had been successfully breached. And so, here I was, sitting opposite her in an armchair, determined to withstand any of her onslaught. The girls, an inalienable phenomenon of our surroundings, were playing behind me, squeaking and murmuring relentlessly.

I started first:

"It cannot continue like this any longer! It's just not working! Dimitri must come home!"

"And what will he do here?" - Madam Natela blurted out, squinting her penetrating green eyes.

"And what should I do without him? What kind of family is this?"

My mother-in-law was a very stubborn woman and because of this I expected great resistance from her, but instead of her usual tantrum she suddenly agreed:

"Yes, you're right. It's no good for spouses to be apart for such a long time. And it is no good for my grandchildren either. They need a father."

I was very surprised and glad that she agreed with me so easily but what she said next, made my jaw drop.

"Why don't you join your husband then?"

"What?!"

"Yes, take the girls and go to your husband."

It was such an absurd suggestion that my sister-in-law started impulsively laughing and I couldn't hold back a smile either:

"You're kidding, right?"

"No", - Madam Natela hilariously rounded her lively green eyes, theatrically showing us her frustration that we couldn't see such an obvious thing: - "Dimitri is not coming. It is absolutely out of the question. Then there is only one option left; you should go."

Arguing with my mother-in-law was never a good idea, so Marina and I just smiled again and left her room. But Dimitri's mother was not the type of woman one could ignore so easily and pretty soon I had my lesson taught. In next to no time everybody around me became aware that I was going to America. Even people I barely knew would stop me in the streets and ask:

"When are you leaving, dear?"

"Who told you that? I am not leaving anywhere."

"You aren't? Sorry, our mistake", - they would apologize but in their doubtful eyes I saw that they didn't believe me.

Even our closest friends started questioning my words.

"Don't hide the truth from us. We won't tell anybody."

I got annoyed by the bizarre situation in which I found myself plunged and a few times even argued with my mother-in-law.

"Madam Natela, stop spreading rumors, please. It's getting ridiculous. You know I cannot go to America."

"Why not?"

"Because I don't want to... And even if I wanted to, I couldn't. Do you know how many people are trying to get visas and they cannot? Only one from a hundred gets the American Embassy's approval."

"Nonsense. They won't resist you."

"Why not? Because I'm your daughter-in-law?"

"Hush, girl. Don't get fresh here!"

"Madam Natela, I don't even have an invitation."

"We got it for Dima, We'll get it for you."

"Why are you so desperate to send me overseas?"

"Because your husband needs you there. You see? Soon it'll be a year he has been in America and he still hasn't got things straighten out. It's because he is too soft and too polite and I'm sure everybody is taking advantage of his modest character."

"And in your eyes I'm what? Margaret Thatcher?!"

"Margaret, not Margaret, tougher than my son. What? You don't want to help him?"

"Of course, I do, but we don't have money for that. Whatever Dima is sending is barely enough for food."

"That's fine. If needed, we'll sell our apartment."

"For Goodness sake," – I waved my hands again and left her sight in despair.

Regardless of my resistance, Madam Natela's words still had an impact on me. I didn't want to discuss this matter with her. Instead I started consulting with my sister-in-law. We used to retire to her bedroom and in a half-whisper discuss the current state of our affairs:

"What if I try, Marina? You think it's impossible?"

"With two children? Absolutely out of the question."

"I cannot leave the girls!"

"Of course you can't."

Painful doubts hunted me for almost a month and still I couldn't make any decision.

"What if I try, Marina? What if it works? You know I am better than Dimitri with papers."

"You sure can try but what about an invitation? Are you going to ask those horrible people again?"

Going to the 'office' was not an option.

"I'll do it in my way."

So I did. We hadn't got any American relatives back then but I had and still have a lot of friends from all over the world thanks to my university years and academic connections. So, I contacted one of my old buddies who worked at the Chicago University as a research scientist, and mentioned that I would like to visit America with my daughters for two weeks. After a few days she faxed me an invitation letter which soon became a laughing matter for everybody around.

Our neighbor from the fifth floor and a close friend of the family, Leah, openly told me straight to the face:

"People with money and connections have official invitations signed and sealed by American attorneys with golden seals on them, and still cannot get the Embassy approval and you hope to convince the consular with this funny piece of paper?"

Soon our tiny kitchen turned into some sort of meeting spot. What kind of absurd thoughts its walls did not hear. Not believing that any good could come through my 'piece of paper', people familiar with immigration matters started giving me absolutely unimaginable advices, such as: "Forget about your funny invitation. You should go to Canada first; it's much easier to get a Canadian visa. Then you can drive down to the US." Or even crazier: "Go to Mexico and then walk to America through the desert, we heard it's possible."

I was stunned by such advice; walking through an unfamiliar desert with kids! No thanks; I much preferred dying from starvation at home. But I still had my invitation, sure no 'golden seal' but at least it was authentic and I felt like it was worth to give it a shot. Meanwhile our family became extremely polarized, on one side my mother-in-law enthusiastically cheering for this endeavor, and on the other side my own mother, Madonna, loudly wishing that this entire venture would fail.

And finally the big day approached. I had to look like a respectable and, what was even more important, wealthy lady who in such a disastrous time for Georgians had nothing else to worry about but to go to a foreign country with two lovely kids just for fun. But I faced one big problem: although the girls were still nicely dressed, I had nothing suitable to wear for such a special occasion. All my appropriate clothes were long sold off. That was the time when the incredible openness of Georgian society came in especially handy. As soon as I mentioned my dilemma to my friends, in the blink of an eye I had every necessary tinge to show off. On top of all the other nuances of the wealthy dress code I was trying to mimic I added my aunt Maria's antique jewelry and wrapped myself in a neighbor's beautiful long sable coat made from the winter pelage finest fur, probably more expensive than our apartment. When I looked into a mirror, I was knocked dead.

"Damn it, Marina," – I turned to my sister-in-law, - "I never looked so elegant in my life. Not even when I was the wife of a factory owner. I wish I had more time to get used to all of this luxury. Don't you think it's too much? Do I look fake? I feel a little awkward."

"You'll be fine", - she dismissed my worries with a smile.

The next day we had an appointment at the American consulate but at night Mariam, our youngest daughter, got very sick. She'd been throwing up all night and only by the morning did she feel a little bit better.

Even before the dawn, my parents rushed to our place. Dad remained, as I expected, very optimistic and positive, but my mother was completely beside herself with frustration:

"That's a bad omen! God doesn't want you to leave for America. Cancel the journey. Don't go!" – she pleaded but I was unshakable.

"How do you know that it is God, not the devil trying to ruin our plans?" My poor mom. If only I knew.

So, at the appointed time I went to the Embassy with the girls. We paid our fees and then an embassy employee took us into a huge hall, where about eighty, eighty five visitors were waiting for their interviews. The girls behaved like perfect little ladies, as though realizing how important this day was for our whole future. We were among the last ones and thus witnessed that only few visa-seekers got the consular's approvals before us. All of this didn't look very encouraging at all and my heart started jumping from anxiousness and fear but when our turn came, suddenly everything went unexpectedly, I would say, even mysteriously smoothly.

A consular, an approximately thirty year-old neat -looking guy, quickly browsed through our documents, then he picked the invitation letter among the bunch of papers, cautiously read it and when finished, he politely asked me how I had known the person who was inviting us. I was prepared for this inquiry and presented him a bundle of letters, received from my friend during fifteen years or so of our acquaintance. The consular was seemingly impressed. After that he didn't even look at the remaining documents. He just asked me a few more questions.

"Where do you work?"

"I don't work".

"How come?"- He sounded surprised.

"Because my girls are too small and they need me at home. Besides, there are no good jobs anyway. At my previous job at Tbilisi State University I was getting a salary equivalent to 30 cents in American currency."

"One cannot call it a decent salary,"- the consular shook his head in disapproval.

I agreed with a sour smile and the consular moved on to inquiring information about my husband.

I blushed. I don't know if he noticed it or not but my ears started burning like hell. Now I had to lie to this nice guy and it didn't turn out as easy as I had hoped.

"He is abroad."

"For what purpose?"

"Because there are no jobs here anymore. Nearly half of the Georgian men work in Russia or Ukraine nowadays."

I was painfully awaiting for the next question which undoubtedly should be about Dimitri's exact whereabouts and I already had a phony document prepared that he worked somewhere in Russia but suddenly the consular put my papers aside, looked at me smiling and announced:

"That's a pity. I would give him a visa too."

I couldn't believe my ears.

"Are you giving us visa approvals?"

"I certainly am."

I was so shocked that for the moment couldn't move and became completely speechless.

"Do you have any further questions?" – The consular asked impatiently because other candidates had been waiting for their turns.

"No, I don't. Thank you," – I barely managed to answer.

I stood up, grabbed my girls' hands and left the hall. I was so bewildered that I even forgot my precious letters. What was that? A joke? I couldn't understand. Did the consular realize that Dimitri was already in America and just pitied us or did I fool him? I often wonder about this mystery till today, but one way or another it was a true miracle for us.

When I came home and told the family what had just happened, it was like a bombshell. Hearing that, my mom's heart sank but everybody else was very happy about it.

"The time will come and you will regret it", - mom told me quietly and reproachfully looked at my father. Until the end of her days, she did not cease blaming my innocent dad for helping me and Dima in the realization of this insane adventure. Forgive me, Mom, for any pain I caused you in this and the next world.

The news spread among our acquaintances quickly. Many of them had been encouraging me to try getting visas but as it turned out only a few had actually believed in its success. Now they all were caught with a huge surprise and started asking me questions about whom we bribed and how much it cost so that they could do the same. I was swearing over and over again that no such kind of thing ever took place but nobody listened to me. Nobody believed in random miracles in embattled Georgia anymore.

"What? You want us to believe that a woman with two children got a visa approval without a bribe? Not a chance!"- That was their overall verdict.

At first I became very upset about all this and tried to pursue the doubters but then I realized that I didn't have time for such nonsense. I had much more important things to take care of and to take care of immediately. We had got visas on January 13th and they would expire exactly in three months. I needed act swiftly and wisely if I didn't want to lose our only chance. But I had no money for the journey. According to the law of meanness, Dimitri was not able to send even a dime during that time period. Knowing that my husband and I would soon be able to pay back, all our friends and relatives were willing to lend me a hand but even then, I managed to collect only one thousand USD in two months, certainly not enough to buy three round-trip tickets to America. I was utterly devastated. Then another miracle happened.

One lucky morning our neighbor from the fifth floor, Leah, dropped in and brought a couple of sweet rolls for our girls. I cut the buns into pieces so that everyone would get it and put on the water to make fresh tea. The children immediately grabbed their portion, as well as a slice for their grandma and ran into her room. Leah sat down on a chair closer to the gas stove.

"Exhausted, utterly exhausted!"

"Why? What's up?"

"Just coming from the bakery and barely got to the house."

"Don't say that there is the problem with flour again!"

"No, thank God, everything is quiet there, but you should have seen what's going on at the exchange booth! Barely snuck through the frenzied crowd."

"It's weird. I thought no one has cash anymore."

"So it is so, but no one wants to lose those pennies they still have."

"I don't get it."

"Me neither but someone in the queue was explaining to others that at the stock market the American dollar made an enormous jump against the Georgian currency a couple of hours ago and this is why all exchange booths are buying dollars like crazy now."

It felt as if I got an electric shock.

"And how much are they paying for a dollar?"- I asked impatiently.

"Twice as much as yesterday evening."

"This might be our chance, Leah."

"What you mean?"

"They sell tickets only for the Georgian currency at the air ticket office."

I didn't have time for further explanation. I left our astonished guest in the kitchen, grabbed my coat and the purse and jumped out. We lived in the centre of the city and everything was within a ten-minute walk from our house. I ran to the nearest exchange booth, sold all our dollars, and then ran to the travel agent's to buy tickets in Georgian currency. And it worked. I had just enough money for three tickets. How odd was that? What could you call it if not a true sign from heaven?! After that even my mom gave up on her holy crusade against our venture.

Then departure time came; March 16, 1999. Nearly all our family and close friends went with us to the airport, and my mom was among them. She wasn't talking; she was just staring at me with wide, almost crazy eyes. When we passed the custom service and went across the gate, I turned to her and not being able to bear that gaze anymore, told her:

"Mom, stop it. It is not the end of the world. I'll be back in six months, in worst case, in a year."

She shook her head and whispered in a trembling voice:

"No, I'll never see you again."

Regardless of how long I'll live, this painful scene will never fade away from my memory, but back then I didn't pay much attention to it. I was too preoccupied with another matter; a whole new world was waiting for me and my daughters across the ocean and I was worried only about that.

Chapter 3

When our plane landed at O'Hare International airport, America greeted us with beautiful cool weather. It was lightly snowing but no wind or gale as we'd been warned of beforehand about Chicago's harsh climate. We had just gone through a long tiresome flight and the girls were a bit too capricious. I felt nervous myself too but the reason behind it was quite different. I was warned beforehand that even at the destination checkpoint there still might be some unexpected problems, so I had to be watchful. Fortunately, everything went smoothly that time too.

"Welcome to America", - an elderly chubby customs officer greeted us with a friendly smile and stamped my passport in three different places.

When I glanced inside it, I noticed that instead of two-week permeation, he had granted us with six months staying approval. I was so happy. I thanked him sincerely and headed with the girls towards the waiting hall where my friend was supposed to meet us but unfortunately one unpleasant surprise was also awaiting us there: our suitcase didn't arrive at the luggage section. It had disappeared somewhere between Tbilisi – Moscow - Chicago.

"Don't worry. This happens quite often at international airports," - my friend comforted me. – "They must have sent your luggage to some other country. They will find it and bring it to you in a few days."

It still upset me very much because I realized what an unforgivably stupid mistake I had made when I put almost all our documents into that suitcase.

Now if it was gone, that would be a great inconvenience. But could moaning after the fact or crying fix anything? No. So I sucked it up, filled out all the necessary papers for lost and found items and left the airport, putting all my hopes on the Almighty's mercy.

If anyone wishes to see the New World for the very first time, choosing Chicago as a starting point is probably one of the best decisions. But if you get such a cordial host to welcome you and show you around as we did, you may consider yourself not only smart but lucky as well. Our first week in America was just amazing. Without our luggage we faced a serious shortage in clothes but fortunately my friend had a lot of unused new garments of her daughter and she generously presented them to my girls. She found a few jeans and shirts for me too, so this problem was easily fixed. But if this was not enough, the very next day Olga took us to the toy store and bought two beautiful Barbies for Nino and Mariam. The girls were thrilled. They never had such fine-looking dolls before. Personally I was shocked by the price. Each toy cost over fifty bucks.

"That's a lot, Olga. I'm very thankful but you really shouldn't do that. That's a lot of money for a toy," – I protested but she was firm in her decision.

"That's fine. This is their first encounter with a different culture, Tsira. Your girls will never forget this."

And indeed, it made an unforgettable impression. And it was not an isolated case. Our kind host took us to many places. No matter what we were doing, strolling aimlessly about the Loop, as locals call the downtown area, during the pleasant sunny midday or walking in a daze up avenues under the towering night-lit skyscrapers of the Windy City, Chicago managed to amuse us equally. Sure I heard about the famous Chicago architectural school before but seeing all these impressive monuments with my own eyes was an absolutely spectacular experience. From the first steel-framed high-rise structure, the Home Insurance Building, to America's two tallest towers, Willis Tower and Trump International Hotel, I was deeply interested in everything. Most parts of the days we spent touring around the various parts of the city, entertaining ourselves by observing the dazzling Loop, the picturesque scenery of the lakefront neighborhoods and the unforgettable panorama of Lake Michigan itself, the Chicago suburb of Oak Park, were my friend's family lived, and many other upscale establishments. Much smaller details than skyscrapers also caught my eye. For example: the wide streets of the residential areas with ample patches of grass or trees that separated the roads from the sidewalks reminded me of Tbilisi. We have the same street patterns but not in such a huge scale, of course.

In the evenings we dined at one of the famous ethnic restaurants Chicago is so abundant with. Polish Patches, Little Seoul, Chinatown and many other colorful districts; they all had something unique and unforgettable to offer to the wondering tourists. Actually, we tasted so many unusual cuisines during our first week in America that I had an impression that we were visiting not one but many foreign countries in one fell swoop. The multiculturalism and diversity of the Wind City were the most remarkable things that pleasantly struck my curious mind.

As for the girls, the grand achievements of the modern architecture kept them amused only for a couple of hours. After that they didn't pay any attention to the skyscrapers. They were more occupied with staring at the people. They knew about the existence of many different races only through TV and now live materialization of this virtual knowledge became as if they themselves plunged into the discovery channel. An unusually big number of overweight people also had a notable impact on them as well as on me, but pretty soon they got used to this novelty too and stopped gazing at strangers.

Kids! Nothing is able to impress them for long, but Chicago's one jewel still overcame their young skeptical nature - Shedd Aquarium with its rich Oceanarium, amusing aquatic show and Polar Play Zone totally won their hearts. Nino and Mariam had been bearing the cheerful memories of that magical place in their minds for many, many years.

Unfortunately, any merry time comes to its end sooner or later. So, while we were sitting in the Lavalza Espression Cafe at the John Hancock Observatory, enjoying a breath-taking sunset view from the top of this American architectural icon and sipping excellent dark coffee, I informed my friend that we would be leaving her hospitable home the next morning.

"Tomorrow? But it's been only one week. I thought you'd be staying with us twice as long."

"A good guest is one who never fails to leave in time," – I joked.

"What? You didn't like it here?"

"Of course we loved everything here, but I want to visit New York for a couple of days as well. I'll exchange our return tickets and we'll fly home from JFK."

This news didn't please Olga, although she was not completely surprised. I had at least a dozen friends in NY and my wish to visit them too sounded quite logical. Nevertheless she still tried to convince me to stay in Chicago anyway.

"Your luggage hasn't arrived yet. Besides, there are so many great things you should see here. I was planning to take you to the Joffrey Ballet."

It's not easy to impress a Georgian with hospitality as we ourselves are quite known for this trait. And still our host's cordiality deeply touched me, but only after years, when I learned on my own how hard it is for Americans to find free time on behalf of others, manage busy schedules or skip work, not to mention the cost of all these selfless actions, did I fully appreciated Olga's generosity.

I realized that getting into a Greyhound bus and heading toward New York was like burning bridges behind us. Shamelessly fooling a trustful friend was not a deed one should be proud of either. By doing this I unwillingly crossed an invincible border of cordial, welcoming America and stepped into total uncertainty. The worst part of it – I was dragging my kids with me. But the girls were not aware of any of such matters. They only knew that in a couple of days they would meet their daddy and were very excited about it. Mariam, the younger one, was prattling all the way nonstop, burying me in endless questions. Nino, my older one, was mostly quiet and I explained this unusual calmness by the mere fact that she was sitting on the other side of the aisle and simply was not able to get to me so easily. I only learned about the real reason hidden behind her exceptional behavior years later when Mariam confessed that Nino had been scared to death of the huge African-American passenger who was sitting beside her. Not an example of perfect parenting I am picturing to you here, I reckon, and I can only justify my carelessness by saying that being always open-minded to new things myself and not very experienced as a mother I shamefully failed to realize the danger hidden behind a rough encounter with a new and unfamiliar world for the unprepared mind of my nine year-old child. No doubt, it's a great thing to make the youngsters' inner world wider by introducing fresh things but this should have been done in a more careful, softer way, preferably through children of their age. Thankfully, no permanent harm was done to my daughter's psyche. Eventually she overcame that incident without any tinge of xenophobic fear and, now having a lot of Afro-American friends, she only laughs when remembering that stupid incident.

As for me, I enjoyed the company of that loud and humorous African-American guy very much. The whole way to NY he was joking non-stop about various things and from time to time stridently argued with me that Mariam's obvious African features automatically led to the conclusion that my boyfriend or husband was undoubtedly black and for some unknown reason I was not admitting that. My rock-solid argument that in Georgia there were no colored men available and even if I'd wished, I probably wouldn't have been able to find one, meant nothing to our witty companion. All this was a joke, of course, and made me laugh a lot but also gave food to my thoughts as well. Having a small, straight, Russian nose, Mariam still has very unique looking big black eyes, quite unusual for the white race. Could it be true that she has some African blood in her veins? Well, theoretically it's possible. I come from Abkhazia. My mom and dad both hale from that breakaway part of Georgia. And from history lessons I remembered that thousands of years ago some Egyptian pharaoh had brought Ethiopians with him to Colchis, which is today's western part of Georgia. Many of them stayed there and eventually vanished, fully assimilating with the local tribes. But it was so long ago. Could it be true that my annoying and noisy American pal from the Greyhound bus was sensing that hint of common gene in Mariam's eyes? It's funny but the fact is, none of us actually knows which genes we all carry in our blue veins.

Chapter 4

Maybe The Big Apple really is a dream city for most people from around the world but when we first arrived there, I didn't feel the slightest desire to stay there even for a couple of hours. Everything looked so scary and so confusing to me. So many people around and everybody was rushing somewhere. My only thoughts were do not lose the children and keep them safe. As soon as we came to the central bus terminal, I grabbed Mariam's hand and as my another hand was dragging our suitcase, kindly bought for us by Olga, I instructed Nino to walk directly in front of me, so I could always see her. I found a ticket office and purchased the earliest passes to Springfield, MA, as for that moment, Dimitri lived in that area. I felt little bit released only when we got onto the bus and were headed for Massachusetts. After several days of being on the road the girls were already exhausted but still looked very excited. So did I and no wonder why; in a few hours our family would be reunited again and I was very anxious about that.

It took four hours or so to get to the destination point. Finally, our bus made a brief stop at the local terminal and we got out of the vehicle. Dimitri was already there, waiting for us, but I was hardly able to single out my chubby hubby among the medley crowd of rushing people. Lean and a bit bristle, he looked so different in his tight blue jeans and loose unbuttoned black top over a white t-shirt.

"Hi, handsome," – I smiled and kissed his unshaved cheek. – "Have you behaved well in my absence?"

Dimitri blushed and glanced around with his huge azure eyes. It was funny, because he was thirteen years older than me but still acted like a child and even the slightest display of passion between us in public made him extremely uncomfortable. "You, women, are shameless", - it was his favorite quote in such situations but I never paid any attention to it because I knew that deep inside he secretly loved when I showed fondness for him.

The girls were thrilled, jumping around their daddy and trying to climb his legs. Then we all got into Dimitri's car and drove away. It was an old red Opel that suspiciously coughed and shook at every single red light but we still fell in love with it because it was our first vehicle in America.

Soon we arrived in the tiny city called Chicopee. Dimitri, with his companions, had been renting a three bedroom apartment on the second floor of the two storey run-down building on Cabbot Street. When we arrived there, I couldn't believe what I saw. The place was literally filled with people of different nationalities, all from the former USSR with the exception of one guy who was from Poland. No furniture, nothing, just mattresses everywhere except for the kitchen where they still possessed a dirty sink, a stinky counter, and an old rocky table with a few shabby chairs. As for the filthy bathroom, you don't want to hear about that.

Tenants met us with reticent cordiality. They were not unfriendly or hostile, just restrained which was actually a very good thing because one doesn't wish more forthcoming enthusiasm from a constantly boozy bunch of strangers. There was not enough space to give us a separate room so we shared one with a Russian guy named Ruslan. There were no spare beds for us either but the tenants from the Baltic republics kindly bestowed to us the bottom part of one of their mattresses. The hard pad with a wooden frame and broken springs loosely dancing inside it sure couldn't make a comfortable bed for anybody, however it was less contagious, at least I hoped it would be, and this thought consoled me a little bit.

From the very first minute as our feet touched the ground of that typical skid row I knew that no child belonged there. I was terrified. Nevertheless, I didn't say a word of complaint to Dimitri because this would bring me nothing but despair. Instead, I started thinking how to get out of this quagmire. It was no easy dilemma to solve, especially in our situation, with no permanent status of residency or any money in our pockets. One thing I couldn't understand was why anybody in his/her right mind would choose such a miserable place to live, but pretty soon I got an answer - almost all of our roommates, except for two Lithuanians, were illegal aliens.

You, my kind reader, are probably not too surprised to hear this, as immigration problem has already got a lot of publicity and attention lately but then, almost two decades ago, it was different for me; it was a complete shock and the reason of this partially lied in my Soviet background. Back, in the communist era, in the USSR, rules of residency were so strict and harsh even for natural citizens, never mind foreigners, that moving from one part of the country to another, particularly to the capital-cities or big industrial centers, required special permission from the government. When we hosted foreign guests, we could only take them within twenty five kilometer radius from our houses. Illegal aliens? We hadn't even heard about such weirdness. We didn't face dilemma of illegality in newly established independent Georgia either, although the reason for this was exact opposite of the USSR's. Georgia has extremely liberal immigration laws, I would say too liberal, and to become a legal citizen of my country is quite easy for anybody with a clean criminal background.

Therefore, in the run-down apartment on Cabbot Street, the problem of illegality emerged as an utterly unfamiliar issue for us, but I quickly got the message and started thinking about how to avoid that quite a dangerous trap. Our first call was Dimitri's new boss, of course. At that moment my husband worked for a Polish guy named Tadek M., who was a fresh immigrant himself, married to an American girl, and now owned his own cleaning company. Many East Europeans worked for him, most of them illegals. When Tadek learned that Dimitri was not happy about joining the army of undocumented aliens and was planning to proceed with his legal actions to get a work permit, he promised to help but, as life proved it, he appeared to be the king of procrastination. For any of our needs or requests he always had one answer: 'Sometime next week.' I cannot really say if it was his raison d'être or it was just a classical case of irresponsibility but we just wasted so much time waiting for his help in vain.

Dimitri was a very reserved and insightful person and always did his best not to be too pushy, which was not necessarily a bad thing, I suppose, but under certain circumstances this kind of extra tenderness really could ruin one's life, and it was accurately our case. We were trapped with Tadek. In order to keep going, we needed at least some money, and without a work permit he was our only source of income. Unlike my husband, I felt that we had to be more persuasive in convincing his employer to help us. I was not completely dumb and I already realized that it was not just our ill fate that kept Tadek from taking steps in the right direction. As usual, it was about money. For an average employer it was just much more profitable to have illegal slaves than legal employees to whom he had to pay a decent salary, plus give all benefits in accordance of the state law. But I still felt like we had a chance. I knew that Tadek liked Dimitri and respected him, so against all odds he still might help us. In such a situation I should probably have taken action into my own hands and pushed our case a little harder but I was a Georgian wife and jumping before one's husband was not exactly our tradition.

We were cornered in a dead end so badly that I started to fear that we might be stuck in that sorry place for a really long time. And then boom, sudden help emerged from a totally unexpected source. It was that rarest case when one could thank God for granting him/her with snoopy neighbors. To make a long story short, in the same building where we lived, some elderly couple was renting an apartment. They noticed the children and found it extremely suspicious that two little girls had been living with a bunch of strange guys, and they started complaining about it. The couple even threatened one of our Lithuanian tenants that if the necessary steps wouldn't be taken immediately in the welfare of the children, they would notify the authorities. O, boy, you should have seen what an amazing impact those angry words from the two skinny old folks made on our beefy roommates. It scared the crap out of them. That very day somebody called the boss, and Tadek, who never had spare time for us, popped by right away. At the emergency meeting everybody agreed that a solution should be found without delay. During the negotiations I mentioned in a Quasi-inadvertent manner that our family could move out and live somewhere else if only we had money. Tadek loved the idea, so did the others. They wanted to get rid of us so badly that one of them even landed us money to make it happen.

As a result, in no time we got our first apartment in America in the outskirts of the urban town called Springfield. Thus, we became somewhat like the Simpsons' family from the famous cartoon series, and our girls loved that resemblance. Dimitri and I also noticed the similarity but not in a good way- it felt as if something phony, something surreal, like cartoon settings, substituted our real life.

I can't quite recall who helped us to rent the apartment. Probably it was Ruslan, our roommate, who knew someone in the local real-estate business. For that time I still had my valid white card which proved that the girls and I could legally stay in America for almost five more months. Therefore renting an apartment didn't cost us any problems, but we stayed in our first dwelling place only for a month as the utility bills appeared to be way too expensive for our modest income.

Meanwhile I was in persistent communication with the lost and found department of Aeroflot, fruitlessly searching for our vanished suitcase which never resurfaced again. But later it turned out that even such a misfortune was not so bad for us after all. As I mentioned before and probably will repeat it over and over again, sometimes God really acts in mysterious ways, at least in our case. So, although we never got our luggage back, instead we received six-hundred-dollar compensation from the aviation company, which was a really handsome imbursement for us at the time. With such a solid sum in our pocket we could buy a used car but in order to do so we needed an American driver's license which we didn't have. And once again, a Good Samaritan popped up to help. Some new friend enlightened us with the useful suggestion that instead of a Massachusetts driver's license we should seek an international one which would be even better because it would work in all of the states.

Ordinary Americans may wonder how foreigners can get their hands on these kinds of documents. Very easily, my friends, one should just browse through the foreign language tabloids of the Big Apple, and will find tons of advertisements of law offices which are more than happy to help a newcomer to get a work permit, a social security card or a driver's license. (At least, it was this way in the late 1990s).

Once we read such appealing promotions, I asked my husband:

"Doesn't it sound too good to be true?"

"How do I know?" He shrugged his shoulders.

Then we consulted about the matter with Dimitri's co-workers and they assured us:

"Come on, guys. It's America. Everything is different here. It seems odd only for us, newcomers. In reality, Americans hate routine and bureaucracy. They make everything quicker and easier here. Even Green Cards we get by regular mail."

Getting documents of permanent residency by mail! We were impressed. Truly a land of wonders! we thought. But we still had some doubts.

"If it is so easy, why doesn't everyone do it? Why are there so many illegals here?"

"Well... I don't know. Maybe because most of them are Mexicans and they don't really need papers,"- the friend suggested. – "They are seasonal workers, you know. They come and go whenever they want."

"Come on!"

"Yeah, yeah. It's true. Down, in the southern states, all crop businesses are thriving on cheap Mexican labor. This is why food products are so cheap In America. You didn't know that?"

Wow! Totally unsecured borders! Who could expect such flamboyant extravaganza from the mighty country? Back in the Soviet era, the border patrol would interrogate even migrant birds about their purpose of entering our sky, never mind letting in myriads of seasonal workers. Now, facing the opposite extreme of complete looseness from another superpower also made us feel quite puzzled, but again, who were we to question the actions of mighty countries. So, we didn't over- analyze the reasons behind all of that peculiarity. We just started thinking how to personally benefit from that circumstance. So, we followed the instructions given in the tabloid ads and sent copies of our passports and Georgian driver's licenses along with the required fees to one of the afore-mentioned law offices. And indeed, in a couple of weeks we received our work permits, social security cards, and driver's licenses by mail.

It was a joyful moment for our family. We immediately left our pricey apartment in Springfield and moved to another one. This time our new home was situated in the tiny city of Indian Orchard. By the way, we were surprised to find that changing cities in that part of America is rather a symbolic act than an actual one because there are no borders between adjacent cities. It's just one big urban area, and that was also a novelty for us. In New England a traveler could drive from one city to another without ever noticing any difference between them, while in Georgia, even small villages are separated from each other with open fields or mountains.

Now, back to my story. In Indian Orchard, we rented a two bedroom apartment on the first floor of a two story private house. It was an almost two century-old run down building, owned by some ex-congressman or senator of Polish descendant. The apartment itself was no good at all, with color-faded rotten carpet floors, squeaky doors and crooked screen-less windows, all spottily covered in ex-white-now-turned-gray, lead-contaminated paint. The dirty walls and huge holes everywhere didn't make the place more desirable either, but along with all that kind of malady it also had several irreplaceable advantages: First of all, the apartment was ridiculously cheap, only two hundred bucks per month which included electricity and water payments. Secondly, it was spacious and the girls finally got their own bedroom. The house also had a large grassy front yard and a shady orchard behind the house, hidden from curious onlookers by a tall bushy hedge, so we could rest now and then out there. One more pro, worthy to mention -the whole neighborhood was rather poor but very friendly, quite safe and well protected, thus the girls could enjoy outdoor activities sometimes as well. And finally, last but not least, our landlord, Mr. Stanley, an elderly, skinny, tall man with firm, sharp features, although being all rough, acrimonious, always grumpy, and not very choosy with his language, still was fairly sympathetic towards newcomers, often mentioning that he remembered well the hard days his immigrant parents had been through while trying to find their niche in their new homeland. I have a suspicion that our symbolic rent payment was more humanitarian support than actual payment. He also helped us with maintenance problems in every possible way he could.

   Mr. Stanley was not the only one who helped us out in Indian Orchard. I don't know how the locals had found out about the shortage we had been experiencing in clothes because of the loss of our luggage, but the very next morning after our arrival in the new place, I found two huge plastic bags sitting in front of our main entrance, full of brand new clothes for me and for the girls. We were astonished but as it turned out, it was only the beginning. Countless strangers literally rushed to help us out in solving many different issues. I will not annoy you by recalling every single detail of our adventures. I'll just tell you that very soon we had everything necessary to make a decent living: we had clothes, we had furniture, we had toys for the kids, and all these we had for free, but most importantly, we gained new friends with many of whom we maintain quite warm relationships till today.

   I've just said that I'm not going to plunge into every detail of our daily struggles but I still want to share a few little episodes with you because I think that some of you, who care about immigration problems, may find it interesting to look at this issue from the other side's prospective as well. Here comes one occurrence that still remains fresh in my mind.

   When the beginning of a new school year approached us, Dimitri and I faced one absolutely inevitable dilemma; we had to enroll our girls in the public school system. Fortunately, as it turned out, the child protection law of the USA indiscriminately guarantees the basic education rights for any child on American soil, regardless of the parents' legal status; thus, that particular problem of ours was resolved relatively easily. As for our children - Nino, the third grader, seemed quite happy about going to new school, meeting new friends, while Mariam, who knew no English what-so-ever, had never been at school before and, what made her situation even worse, was a shy person by the nature, became increasingly nervous because of all of the novelty suddenly facing her. In the Massachusetts' public schools system they have a special program for foreign children who don't speak English and bilingual teachers help them to blend into their new environment. But we were from tiny country and, understandably, no one knew the Georgian language among those teachers. However, that little inconvenience didn't stop the school bureaucracy to provide us with help anyway, not in Georgian but in Spanish instead. The situation was almost comical but not for Mariam, of course. When, after all preparations, I finally brought her to elementary school and was about to leave her there in care of her teacher, my poor baby gazed at me terrified and silent tears poured from her wide, pleading eyes. She looked so miserable, so unhappy. Her caregiver was also seemingly moved by the child's pitiable condition but a minute later her motherly instincts kicked in and she quickly found the simplest and most natural solution.

"That's okay, my little one. You don't understand my words but you'll surely understand this," - she said, warmly snuggling her silently sobbing new charge.

I'll never forget that heartwarming scene, so natural, so sincere, without even a tinge of fake professional politeness.

I don't know if most immigrants experience similar treatment, or if we'd just been especially lucky, but almost all of the eleven years that we spent in the States, we always felt the same genuine kindness and care from Americans.

Anyway, back in the nineties, the American economy was still flourishing and people had no problems finding jobs. Thanks to my working permit and some help from one of our new friends, I too was able to get a job at a local publishing company. But first I had to overcome one obstacle. Dimitri, being convinced that it was only a man's responsibility to financially support the family, was absolutely against it. So, one morning, when, after a tiresome night shift in Kmart, Dimitri was sound asleep, I literary sneaked out the bedroom, stole our Buick Regal, and headed to work. It was quite a risky step from my side because I had never had much experience in driving to begin with, and after so many years without any practice, my self-confidence was even further shaken, but thankfully everything ended without any complications that day. When I came back, Dimitri was awake and furious. But soon he realized that I wasn't about to give up my dreams, so he had to back off. He just growled for a while, comforting himself:

"OK, go for it. You won't be able to bare it more than one week anyway. I bet my life on it."

But I did - I stayed there nearly a month, although it was not easy, I must confess. My new job only had a nice title, 'a publishing company', but in reality, it had nothing to do with actual publishing, at least not in the department where I worked. It was more of a conveyer type job, very tough and tiresome, which didn't required any intellect or knowledge but only unbelievable speed, lots of endurance and physical strength in order to lift heavy stuff. I am a petite woman, weighing a hundred pounds at most, without any hint of strong muscles in my body. Of course, I was not fit for such tasks. It was clear that if I wouldn't come up with some solution, I would simply die or would be kicked out from the company as a completely useless worker and Dimitri would win the bet. And thus, never revealing my troubles to the household, I started looking for a more suitable job. I should mention here that I'm quite good at sewing and this skill helped me find jobs quite easily. Firstly, I moved to an auto craft company which produced slip-covers for cars, and later to a sportswear design company. As a reason for frequently changing employers, I always named low salaries, and it was partially true. I started my American career with the state's minimum wage at the time, $5.25 per hour, but by the time we left the U.S., I was making forty bucks per hour. But there was still a long way to go till then.

But let's not skip ahead and stick with the chronological order. Almost right after I found my first job in America, Dimitri finally freed himself from the cleaning company and this is how it happened. When Dimitri worked in Kmart, thievery was rampant among his co-workers. Dimitri had many quarrels with them about this issue, only to be ridiculed in return. As it was later revealed, he was not the only one who clapped eyes on this and many of the culprits were caught on the security tapes as well. Soon the whole group of cleaners was summoned to the office. The administration knew that Dimitri had nothing to do with the thievery and never accused him of that but during the interrogation it also surfaced that most of the cleaners didn't have proper documents. And what do you think happened next? Nothing really. Instead of calling the police, the administration kicked the whole team of the cleaners out of work without paying a dime for the last two week's work and that was the end of the story. The manager explained his actions by saying that if he called the police, then Dimitri would also face deportation and he/manager didn't want to sacrifice the good man because of some scoundrels. Nobody complained because of it, of course.

Losing the job didn't upset Dimitri even a bit. He had already gotten a work permit, so pretty soon he found another one. For a short time he worked at the local lumber before he got accepted at the big corporation of Milton Bradley where he stayed till the very end.

Chapter 5

When the first year of our arrival in America came to the end, we, as the most of other ordinary residents of the USA, filed our tax papers and after a while even got the tax return check from the state's revenue department. But later we received a letter from the federal revenue office which informed us that they had detected some inconsistency in our documents and asked us to go to the social security office and fix the problem. It was so confusing – how could the same documents be O.K. for the state officials and not O.K. on the federal level? We asked the lady who dealt with our tax papers to find out what it was all about and soon we heard very disturbing news from her – our social security numbers were fake. I don't know what kind of forgery it was; were they just totally made up or maybe they belonged to somebody else but such a nuance didn't really matter, our SS numbers were undeniably forged and that meant trouble, the big one, which we had no idea how to fix. The problem is: once you're at odds with the American immigration law, there's no easy way out of it, or more precisely - no way out at all.

Dimitri and I became very depressed as we thought that all our chances to obtain legal residency in America were lost forever, but in a surprisingly short time we were given a second chance. It happened at the very end of Bill Clinton's presidency. A certain category of illegal emigrants who had relevant jobs were given the rare opportunity to obtain work visas. Full of optimism, we turned to immigration lawyers but soon came to the realization that it was not quite so simple to get the right attorney. Most of them were more than happy to start the legal procedure on our behalf but didn't like our recent employers as legitimate work sponsors and asked us to find new ones, preferably in our professional fields, and that was almost impossible in such a limited amount of time. In two occasions we ourselves had serious doubts about the professionalism of the lawyers. One attorney from Springfield showed way more interest in the age difference between Dimitri and me rather than in our case. Another one, from Stratford, proudly announced that he would definitely win the process for us if we had three million dollars. It was so weird. Why would we seek jobs in America if we had that kind of money?

Nevertheless we were able to found the 'right lawyer' in New York, the Russian one, Andrew Lebedev by name. He worked for the specialized immigration law firm Kaganovich & Associates. He was so nice and supportive! But the most attractive thing about him was that he himself was providing clients with the perfect work sponsors. The whole procedure cost more than four thousand bucks; we had to pay for fingerprints, for legal services, penalties for overstaying our visas and etc. Of course, we didn't have so much money but our friends had lent us the required sum and eventually we covered all of the expenses.

For a while, all went well; consecutively we had received all necessary paperwork: the official registration numbers from the immigration service, then the verification about our sponsors from the Labor department, and at the end - the work contracts for Dimitri and me. But one day the unthinkable happened – the 9/11 terrorist attack. We were as shocked and horrified as any normal human being should. Later we learned that that despicable act of violence directly threatened our family members' lives too. At the moment of the treacherous attack on World Trade Center, Dimitri's sister, Marina, and her newlywed husband Jerry were in one of the twin buildings and narrowly escaped death. For quite a time we couldn't think about anything else but this horrific event but, as life goes on, after a while we all returned to our own affairs. That's when we discovered that our lawyer had disappeared without a trace. We did everything in our power to locate Mr. Lebedev's whereabouts but with no luck. Sensing the rat, we asked one of our friends to call the authorities and find out at what stage our case was. So he did and after a few minutes we knew that neither the Immigration and Naturalization office nor the labor department had ever received any appeals on our behalf from Mr. Lebedev, so our personal registration numbers in their files and all documents supposedly received by Mr. Lebedev from them were just falsifications. I still keep copies of those documents as priceless relics of my own stupidity, and now I briefly explain why I blame only myself.

The thing is that, when the very first time we went to Mr. Lebedev's office, at Lincoln Building 60 East 42nd Street Suite 718 New York, I had spotted the name 'Lebedev' on another door on the same floor that Kaganovich & Associates' office was located. The first thing what had flashed in my mind was that such a stunt could be used by a cheater if he/she wanted to turn a scam here and go unnoticed but I immediately brush off the seditious thoughts. Why on earth did I do that?! I don't know. Perhaps because it was only our second year in America and I was so sick and tired from a decade-long endless list of failures that I desperately needed a break, even at the expense of self-deception. So, as the saying goes, 'If you fool me once... and if you fool me twice'... But what's the point in moaning about it now? I very much deserved all of the consequences that followed after my stupidity but not my poor family, not them! So, my advice to everybody who reads these lines - always find the courage to face reality and never fool yourself; burying your head in the sand never brings any good, it never does.

As for our 'lawyer', only several years later we learned that Andrew Lebedev had been caught and put in jail for similar frauds that he had done to many other immigrants. But the well-deserved punishment of that rascal didn't improve our situation even a bit. We had lost our chance for a long-long time.

Almost every following year, eager to fix our messed up case, we persisted in going to different lawyers but each time we were advised to stay low. All our American friends were encouraging us to stay hopeful and keep trying. So we did. And don't you think that only our close friends treated our immigration problem with such understanding. Quite often even people whom we barely knew or sometimes didn't know at all showed the same kindness in the most unexpected situations. I'll recall only one such episode as an example: Once Dimitri and I were stopped by the police while driving in the city of East Longmeadow. Nothing serious, the cop just wanted to check an expiration date on our windshield sticker and as the common procedure requires it, asked for a driver's license and the technical documentation of the vehicle. You should have seen the officer's face when he saw Dimitri's international driver's license and the foreign passport with an expired guest visa in it. He squatted down beside our rolled down window and gazed at us in full prostration. Then he started scolding us saying that we shouldn't put the police in such an awkward position. He complained that he couldn't even fine us, because if he did so, we would be in big trouble and he didn't feel it was right thing to do. Of course, the officer also advised us to take care of our papers, but how exactly to do that he also had no idea, as nobody else in the entire country, including the people close to the government.

    Once we even contacted Senator Ted Kennedy's office and on another occasion we met with the state congressman's aid. I must admit that all of those officials were quite sympathetic towards us and sincerely wished to help us but unfortunately our problem exceeded their authority. Everybody kept on explaining to us that although technically we were not 'illegals' but 'unwelcomed aliens' (whatever difference between these two terms is,) we still could be deported from the U.S.A. so the only thing what we could do was to wait for a better time or get divorced and find nice American spouses, as we were advised half-jokingly. By the way, a phony marriage is quite a frequent way out among illegal immigrants and it's a very expensive solution as well. Rumor has it that nowadays it costs about twenty-thirty thousand bucks. Once, in a circle of close friends we had even been offered such desperate assistance and completely free of charge, as a matter of fact, but we rejected it partly because we didn't wish to resort to such an awkward solution and partly because it was bad enough that we had already been at odds with the law and we didn't wish to drag our loyal friends into a pit of dubious ventures as well.

Chapter 6

But not everything what we had done during our stay in America was such a vivid error of judgment. Our financial situation, for example, was steadily improving and by the end of the second year, we were able to move to a new place, a two-storied house in the lovely city of Ludlow. Our latest landlords, Joe and Irena, were a very nice couple and pretty soon we became good friends with them. Our neighbors were quite awesome too, especially an elderly couple who lived right next to us. Sadly, we barely saw the wife; she was sick and because of that, stayed mainly indoors, but her husband used to spend a lot of time with our children; he played with them, talked with them, and treated them with candies. The couple had a lot of useful trinkets, watercolor paintings, crayons and stuff like that, leftovers from their grown up children and they gladly shared all those treasures with our girls. Later, they even presented us with four almost brand new bicycles. It was so kind of them and so handy for us. Sometimes we could ride together about the neighborhood as a whole family. After a while we became acquainted with their boys, men to be more correct, who lived somewhere else but used to come to visit their parents fairly often. The couple also owned one extremely seductive thing which lured our girls like a magnet; they had a dog, a very old one, which was so blind that it needed a help to move about the yard, which our girls gladly did. All our family members are big animal lovers actually, so Dimitri and I were very happy that our daughters were given the chance to quench their thirst for playing with a four-legged friend. But pretty soon they got their own pet and this is how it happened.

   Our landlord's wife, Irena, had a kidney surgery and had to stay in bed for a while, and Joe had to work day and night to support his family. It was no surprise that after some time, the poor woman became very lonely. The couple lived in the nearby city of Palmer, and I used to visit Irena almost every other day, but obviously it was not enough. She often whined, "If only I had a small breed puppy." Irena's birthday was coming up, so Dimitri and I decided to present her with an ardently desired puppy. But soon we discovered that prices for pure breeds were way beyond our reach, and Irena wanted exclusively such a one, therefore, we abandoned our previous plan. But then an unexpected chance popped up. One day, at Dimitri's work place, some woman was sharing her brother's family troubles with her coworkers and Dimitri heard that some time ago the woman's brother had brought a little puppy to his children but when his landlord learned about it, he threatened to throw all of them out of the apartment, unless they got rid of the pet. The family was too broke to move to a new apartment, and now the only hope for the poor puppy was to find a new adapting family for him, otherwise the poor thing would be euthanized.

The story was absolutely heartbreaking, and we immediately came to conclusion that it was our destiny to save the puppy. Therefore, the very next day, in the evening, our whole family headed on to a rescue mission. The neighborhood where Dimitri's coworker's brother lived was rather poor and consisted mainly of African Americans.

This is when we first saw him, our adorable puppy. It was love at first sight. He was sitting in the driveway, closely tied up to the fence with a short rope, and surrounded by a bunch of little black kids, as cute as he himself. When the children spotted a family of strangers coming out of the car and heading towards them, they became seemingly alarmed. I approached the girl squatting next to the puppy and asked her with smile:

"Hi, what's its name?"

But my friendliness didn't calm the girl.

"Onyx," she answered, still anxious.

"Of course, Onyx. What a suitable name," I thought to myself. The puppy, about four-month-old black Labrador with honey-sweet brown eyes, looked so tense and miserable, as if he understood the reason behind our appearance. Meanwhile, the people inside the house must have noticed us. Anyway, pretty soon, a burly, baldish man in his mid-thirties, dressed in a loose gray t-shirt and weather-stained, baggy sweatpants of an unrecognizable color came out from the front door, quickly crossed the yard, and stretched out his hand in greeting.

"Hi, I suppose you're the guys my sister has just called me about."

"Suppose we are," replied Dimitri.

It was a weird meeting, tense and awkward, both sides not very comfortable. From the very first glance it was pretty obvious that our host was quite unhappy about the decision he had to make. And we, especially I, were more puzzled than thrilled by the situation as well. I kept staring at the puppy, not knowing what to say. My suspicious behavior made the man's heart wilted.

"You don't like our Onyx, do you?"

Dimitri, who was totally bewitched by puppy's cuteness and couldn't tear his eyes off of him, didn't notice my puzzlement. This is why the host's words came totally out of blue for him.

"Of course we like him! How can anybody not like such an adorable thing?"

"But your wife..."

Dimitri looked at me, astonished.

"Oh, I like him too, but..." Overwhelmed by guilt, I started to justify myself.

"But what?"

"He is not a small dog," I mumbled.

"Oh, if it's only that..." the host regained some hope, "don't you worry, he won't grow too big. Labradors are medium sized dogs."

"But Dimitri, Irena wants a small one. She might not-"

"Nonsense!" He cut me short. "You hear what this man says? He won't grow big."

To make a long story short, my skepticism was easily overwhelmed by Dimitri's childish enthusiasm, the girls' tearful begging, and the host's heartbreaking assurance that if we didn't take the puppy, he would not have any other choice but to put him to sleep.

After some negotiation, Dimitri paid fifty bucks to the man and with that, the deal was completed. After that we all felt relieved - except for our host's unfortunate children, who couldn't hold back their tears when we took their precious puppy away from them. But what could we do? Life is tough sometimes, especially to the poor.

Onyx was stressed too. The poor thing didn't growl or bite but he looked so frightened and unhappy. No kisses or caresses could comfort him. He peed and pooped and vomited all over the car during the ride but nobody really cared about those small inconveniences.

A few days later, Onyx, all groomed and shampooed as the noblest puppy ever, was pompously presented to our landlady, and Irena was absolutely thrilled by her new pet. She hugged and kissed him over and over again and all evening was entirely preoccupied only by playing with him. Seeing that, I felt relieved and all previous doubts left me. But after a fortnight we got a call from her. Irena explained that because of her post-operational condition, it was extremely difficult for her to look after such a playful and lively puppy and asked us to take him to our house for a while until she would get better. Of course, we agreed and thus Onyx moved to our apartment, only to become an inalienable part of our family till the end of his days. Irena never claimed him back and we, from our side, never tried to remind her about that.

Meanwhile, during his first year of puppy-life, Onyx destroyed everything he could put his paws or teeth on. He chewed our shoes, completely ate such inedible items as a household telephone, and even managed to deal with the Joe's old wooden armchair, which was his deceased mother's, by the way, and was very dear to his heart as a memory. Maybe that armchair was the last straw which broke the camel's back. Regardless, after more than a year of happy life in Ludlow, we were told that our landlord had decided to sell the house and now we had two choices - either buy the house or move to another apartment. As you guess, we couldn't buy any property, so we started looking for a new place.

It was a sad time for us. We loved everything in Ludlow: our calm and neat neighborhood, the cordial people we had befriended, the closeness to our workplaces. Now we had to lose all of those privileges, but despite this, we never regretted adopting Onyx. Besides the fact that he had brought so much joy to our lives, thanks to him, we also learned many such aspects of American life which otherwise we would never have known. We discovered how much ordinary citizens love their pets and how they take care of them. We became frequent visitors of such places as Petco, different veterinary clinics, parks and squares where pets were welcomed.

I think, love for animals might be a hereditary thing. I was raised by a pet loving dad, but he was never able to bring one in our apartment because of my mom's firm objection. He had to satisfy his quench for pets only by keeping them in our country house in Abkhazia, and he continues looking after them till nowadays, despite of all obstacles of post-war disaster in our village. Animals sense dad's devotion towards them and they adore him back for that. I heard that not only our cats and a pooch, but even our neighbors' calves and piglets follow him everywhere, as buddies. That's my daddy Nodari.

Dimitri was luckier than me in this matter. His family actually kept pets in their apartment all the time. I even met one, a Polish shepherd named Cocosha, who lived in their family for sixteen years. It's only natural that after our marriage, we maintained a family tradition. Even during extreme poverty, we sheltered a few stray dogs along with a duck and a chick under our roof. On another occasion we hosted our friend's Caucasian shepherd puppy for several months and once, Dimitri even accepted a house mouse as a pet, to my horror.

Our lifestyle was an exception rather than typical in Georgian society, and we were considered as eccentric or even weird individuals by many of our countrymen, but to tell you the truth, we never cared much about others' opinions of us in this matter. It was a completely different case in the United States, and this is why I am paying so much attention to this side of our immigrant saga. This was also one of the many important experiences we gained while living abroad - the knowledge that there were a lot of people in healthy, well-developed societies who shared the exact same values as us. In America no one actually cared about what kind of lifestyle we were living.

No one was shocked by seeing Onyx in the front seat of our car; no one was blaming us for allowing our kids to sleep with their pet in the same bed. We even made many new friends thanks to Onyx. He was such a beautiful boy that even complete strangers couldn't restrict themselves from petting him. To make a long story short, Onyx soon became an indispensable member of our family and the most spoiled one - that's for sure. Dimitri adored him and Girls were crazy about him, considering him not less than their little brother. As for me, I think I was the closest human to him. He grew up sleeping on my chest as a puppy and even later, when he became a big boy and I couldn't bear his weight, he still kept trying to cuddle up on my chest. Actually, I spent more time with him than with any other member of our family. Dimitri used to have overtimes quite often and stayed at work till midnight. The girls were at school almost all day long and only I, due to my new job, about which I'll tell you later, was stuck at home most of the time. Onyx was my faithful companion during the long lonely days. I have to mention that despite the absence of any special training, he became a perfect house guard for us. I felt completely safe in his presence, and that was not the only benefit we got from him. He was one endless source of joy, always ready to please us when we needed him. For example: I hate eating alone, so he always sat beside me, having snacks from mommy's plate. I used to chat with him about everything and he never failed to listen with such an interest as if he understood every single word I said. It was so funny and touching at the same time. O, how I miss those days, if only you knew.

But every medal has two sides, and while we all enjoyed having Onyx around, it still caused us a lot of trouble. The major disadvantage was the fact that we could not get a decent apartment in a nice neighborhood. In most places, pets were not allowed at all and in the others, the prices were so high that we simply couldn't afford them. But having a dog was our choice and we had to except the consequences. This is how we ended up in Springfield once again.

This time our district was not so safe. On the contrary, it was known as the home of drug dealers and different kinds of thugs, but our immediate neighbors were nice. We rented the first floor apartment in a three-store house. The accommodation above us was occupied by an elderly black couple, so quiet and calm that during half a decade of living so close, we barely noticed them. Occasionally their grandchildren used to visit the couple but even they were unbelievably quiet.

The very next day after our arrival in the new apartment, the tenant from the third floor, Jessica, a young lady of south-west origin, welcomed us with a home-made pie. Such cordiality from a stranger might have astonished us before but by then we had already learned about southerners' heartwarming devotion towards their good old traditions, so we were not totally taken aback by her kindness.

Now, when I am recalling all those tiny details of our life in the USA, I, myself, cannot stop marveling at how incredibly blessed we were, especially in moments of hardship, and moving from one place to another should definitely be counted as one of them.

As almost all of the furniture in the Ludlow house belonged to the landlords, the minute we had left their house, we became as poor as church mice. And again, friends came to our rescue; Tadek, Genya, Zdishek, Joe, Pat... the list could last so much longer. Some of them brought the beds, others donated china. Soon we had the most necessary stuff.

One more disadvantage we faced during that time was not having a car. I'll tell you briefly how we had lost our previous vehicle. A few months earlier, one Saturday morning, when I was on my usual journey to Irena's house, who was still in bed after the surgery, I got in a car accident. It was a sunny winter day; all the surroundings, covered in deep snow from the previous night, were shining with dazzling whiteness. Everything was so beautiful, so serene. All the main roads were already cleaned, but still very icy. I was driving slowly, about thirty five miles per hour, enjoying the beauty of the perfect, sunny morning when, suddenly, I heard a blast and my car started hurling from side to side. I got scared and hit the brakes. What happened next, you can easily imagine. I completely lost control of vehicle. Thank God it was a Saturday morning and nobody was on the other side of the road because my old Buick Regal was making such unbelievable pirouettes that a deadly crash would have been absolutely inevitable. At one point it jumped off the snow-covered bordure, like off a springboard, and I literally saw its front wheels rotating in the open air and ice-covered surface of the lake glaring beneath them, but in the blink of an eye, I was on solid ground again, making zigzags on both sides of the road. At last, somehow, I managed to regain control of the wheel and continued driving slowly. I guessed that something was wrong with my car because I could hear weird noises coming from its bonnet but I wasn't sure how serious it could be. I desperately needed some help. I had no doubt about that. But I didn't have a cell phone then and I was not in a residential area, so I continued driving slowly, praying in my heart that the car didn't die until I would find some help. To my relief, after a few minutes, I saw a house, not far from the main road. I stopped the vehicle and went toward the house but was not able to come close to it as there was a huge dog running through the driveway and barking menacingly at me. I was quite scared but still called for help but nobody answered, so I went back to my car to continue the search for another house. But when I tried to start the engine, it failed to start. I got very upset. What could I do?

I waited a while. A few cars passed by, not paying any attention to me, but then one of the drivers stopped and asked if I needed help. I explained my situation to the lady on the wheel and she promised to call the police. I was taken aback. Why should she call the police when I clearly needed a mechanic? Besides that, I didn't have much trust towards law officers in general, thanks to their awful reputation back in Georgia, where, in most cases, they were nothing but criminals in uniforms. So, subconsciously, I didn't expect any good from them in America either. I knew I hadn't done anything wrong but a sudden panic attack still fully overwhelmed my emotions for a while. Then I pulled myself together and silently asked God:

"I commend my fate in your hands, O Lord. Thy will be done as you wish," and started waiting what would come next.

Then another miracle happened. Not in Americans' eyes, perhaps as for them it could feel like a pretty normal thing, but for me, it was a true miracle. The cops arrived and nothing bad happened. They were all polite, calm, and even friendly; no yelling, no screaming, no signs of any kind of intimidation. I didn't realize then but that was the turning point in my life in regaining my trust towards law enforcement. Later I've learned from other immigrants as well that many of them experienced exactly the same thing when they first met American cops face-to-face. Even when they were caught for some sort of unlawful activities, they still noticed that the police were not some kind of above-the-law unit in the U.S.A. and officers there were bound by the law as anybody else. Those kinds of things help us, immigrants to realize that if the justice system works in America, it can work in our countries as well.

In my case the policemen were even kinder than regulations required from them. As I learned later, during the accident I'd hit the electric pole and hadn't stayed at the site because I had no idea about it. While preoccupied by saving my life from falling into the frozen lake, I bumped into so many firm things, probably bordures, that the actual collision simply escaped my notice, but I have to admit that even if I had noticed it, I probably wouldn't have stopped the car for two main reasons: first of all, I didn't know then that the law requires you to stop wherever an accident happens, and second, I was so scared of men in uniforms that I would probably have panicked and tried to avoid facing them anyway. Meanwhile, the cops ran my driver's license through their computer, and then they checked my car and came to the conclusion that, most likely, the burst front tire of the vehicle caused the collision. I was very upset but the cops, instead of pulling out the handcuffs, just scolded me a little for leaving the scene of the accident, and then one of them simply asked:

"Where would you like us to bring you, ma'am?"

I was hardly able to murmur Irena's address. Later Joe often joked about that unfortunate accident of mine, making fun of my fears and repeating over and over again that even in the worst scenario, if cops had arrested me, he and Irina would simply have bailed me out for a couple of hundred bucks and that would be it.

You may be thinking now why I'm paying so much attention to such a mere event and what it has to do with the immigration issue itself, but this is the way we, foreign aliens, experience your culture, and those are the stories we tell to our countrymen about America when we're back home; this is largely how the image of the biggest superpower is conveyed outside of its borders, and those are the bricks that build the real defense wall for your security, not your military strength or the presence of American soldiers all over the world. The true democracy, the strong economy, the fair justice system, the reliable welfare of common citizens, the advanced technologies in service for the benefits of the ordinary people - those are the pillars the America's image stands upon, and when we, foreigners, return to our countries we try to implement them in our everyday lives. This is how democracy and progress should spread over the world, not by using force or by flexing one's muscles. But I'm too off my topic now and it's time to go back to my story.

Now I'd like to open up a little about our faith. Most people would probably agree with the opinion that, regardless of what type of persons we are - hard-line believers, smart-minded agnostics, or downright atheists, our approach to religion always affects our life style, points of view, even the formation of our character. As a family, we belong to the Georgian Orthodox Church, but with a closer look we quite differ from each other. In the matter of faith I deemed Dimitri, my husband, as the strongest one among us, almost the childish type believer, I may say. He didn't know much about religious dogmas or theological teachings and as a matter of fact, he couldn't care less about any kind of formalities but his unconditional love for God and for all his creation far and away outweighed this scarcity of knowledge. He never blamed heaven for any of our troubles and never had any doubts about God's almighty will to save us. My husband's blind and unquestionable faith was so contagious that it had often served us as a lifebuoy in particularly difficult moments of our lives.

As you may have already guessed, unlike Dimitri, I am a classical doubting Thomas type person and therefore constantly suffer from painfully inquisitive thoughts. Although I reckon myself as quite a loyal Christian, I cannot help questioning everything I come upon, especially when it regards faith. Understandably, I read every theological work I can get my hands on, which religion doesn't matter: Christian, Buddhist, Hindu, Muslim, etc… I try discern seeds of truth in every single one of them. I guess our girls took more after me than from their father. Now as grownups, they act in their own ways. Nino, who lives in America, isn't shy to visit different churches of different Christian denominations, and the range of her friends varies from atheists to Native American shamans. As for Mariam, who lives with us here, in Georgia, she is agnostic. I don't approve of my daughters' every step but I strongly believe that faith is a matter that cannot be forced and everybody should find their own way to God, so I try not to interfere.

As I mentioned already, we belong to the Georgian Orthodox Church. Although we had never been devoted church goers in our early years, every now and then we still used to attend liturgical services back in Georgia, especially during the big religious Holidays. So it's only natural that we had a similar urge in America as well. Georgia is such a tiny country that one can hardly find our church outside of our motherland; maybe in huge metropolises like New York or Chicago it's still possible, but in areas like Ludlow or Indian Orchard, forget about that. So we never dreamed of visiting our church in the nearest future but one day, when we still lived in Indian Orchard, while driving through the downtown of Springfield, we noticed a very beautiful church with an inscription on it reading: the Saint George's Greek Orthodox Cathedral. We knew that Georgian and Greek churches are very similar, so we felt like we had found something very dear to us. We immediately stopped the car but even though it was a Sunday afternoon, the building appeared to be closed. It was a big disappointment. Back in Georgia all our churches were opened all the time so we decided that this one was probably not functioning. What could we do? We rubbed its walls lovingly and drove away.

Many months passed after that occasion and we kind of forgot about it. But then Christmas time approached and we recalled that beautiful church once more. I felt very sad that we couldn't celebrate such a beloved holyday in the proper way, so, on December 25th when Dimitri came home after his night shift, totally worn out and sleepy, (If you remember, he worked every single night), I asked him not to waste time on changing his clothes and to take the girls to that church.

"True, it's closed, but at least you can stick candles on its walls," I said.

Dimitri was so exhausted that he hardly could stand on his feet but he loved the idea so much that without any complaint, he took the girls and drove away. Although it was an early winter morning and deep snow covered the road sides, the church was not too far from our place, so I expected them to return within an hour. The time passed by but they didn't come back. I started to worry.

"What if Dimitri fell asleep while driving? What if they had an accident?!" I panicked.

When I finally lost my patience and was ready to call somebody for help, they showed up. You can easily imagine what a joyful moment it was for a terrified mother, but when I learned about the reason of their delay, contradictory feelings stirred my mind: The church we once thought to be permanently closed turned out to be very much functioning and full of merry members and that was excellent news, actually. But the slaphappy step committed by my husband because of it upset me greatly. Seeing the church doors wide open and people going in and out, Dimitri got so excited that, without any second thought, he grabbed the girls' hands and went in. Well, that couldn't pass as a capital crime of course, but still wounded me deeply. The colorful image of three of my beloved ones: Dimitri, in his working clothes, covered in stains and dust after the nightshift, and our angel-like girls, in their less-than-casual dresses, walking into that beautiful church full of festively clad merry people - the classical picture of church beggars, swiftly ran across my eyes.

"What a gaffe!" I moaned frustrated.

I was very down that day but as it turned out, it was one of the luckiest days of our immigrant saga - the day when we finally found our church, or to be more precise, the day our church found us. Here comes a story how it happened. A few days later after the above mentioned event, two pleasant-looking ladies and a man showed up on our doorsteps. I was quite surprised to seeing those smartly dressed strangers in our working class neighborhood.

"Debby, Dorothy and David," they introduced themselves and added that they were members of the Greek Orthodox Cathedral.

Hearing that, my initial bemusement immediately elevated to the level of total embarrassment but shortly I discovered that, despite the fancy appearance of our unexpected guests, they were very nice and cordial people and my unpleasant feelings gradually faded away. It was a landmark moment in our life. From that day on we never felt alone or unwanted. I will not badger you with the long and rotund dithyrambs towards our church because I simply do not have enough words to fully express our gratitude. How could I fully describe the kindness of our priest, Father Chris, and Presbytera Penny, or Father Michael and Presbytera Mary from another Greek church, or other parishioners of the Saint George's Cathedral whose spiritual and sometimes material support was so crucial for us? Instead I plainly testify that if not for the amazing cordiality and support of our church, our life would have never been so pleasant and full of happiness as it was during the entire time of our stay in America.

That blissful day, on behalf of their church, David, Dorothy and Debby invited us to join their communion and, of course, we gladly accepted the invitation.

From that very moment our lives were strongly tied with their community. Although we were not Greeks by origin, we were involved in every aspect of the church life. Sunday services, bible classes, every social event, charity projects, and out-of-state excursions organized by our church, we were always among the most faithful participants of all those activities. We particularly loved the Glendi festival – the annual Greek fair which takes place every first weekend of the month of October. It's a huge event for the entire Greek community of New England. This is why the preparation for it starts way ahead of the actual affair. There is a lot to do for everybody: a lot to plan and calculate for the organizers and a lot to cook for the skilful chefs and their helpers. We belonged to the gang of helpers and mainly participated in selling delicious traditional Greek food, like shpinakopita, suvlaki, musaka and etc. It was a quite tiresome assignment but never drudgery or dull and Glendi was truly worth of all those efforts. By the way, it adds a significant income to our church's budget so we were very happy to be somehow helpful to the amassing community.

Our girls became pretty active participants of church life as well. They joined the gang of Glendi dancers and used to entertain cheerful guests of the festival with fiery Greek folk performances. Later I made the national costumes for the entire dance group, and I'm very pleased to see on the internet pictures the young boys and girls, many of whom I can't even recognize, still dashing in those costumes. But life doesn't consist of only festivals and feasts. Throughout the school year Nino and Mariam used to attend the Sunday school classes and in the summer times they would spend a week or so in the Greek Orthodox camp of the Boston Diocese in New Hampshire. Those kinds of activities had a great impact on forming our girls' characters and I'm tremendously thankful to our church for that.

While talking about faith, I would especially like to emphasize one important topic –religious tolerance. We, Georgians, have been known for a respectful attitude towards people of other faiths from time immemorial, but this only applies to dominant religions, such as Islam and Judaism. However, when it comes to various Christian denominations, unfortunately, passive traits of prejudice often soil our otherwise friendly environment. In America, we have experienced the different approach to this soaring issue. We've learnt how to value the individual rights of a person more than just universally recognized religions'. There is a very large number of religious refugees from the former Soviet Union In New England, and it so happened that we made friends with some of them. We were especially close with one guy, Daniel, and his wife Luba. They both were members of Pentecostal church. Dimitri considered Daniel as his best friend, and our daughters were fond of their five wonderful kids. Luba and I, too, got along very well with each other. Thanks to this couple we got acquainted with many wonderful people from their community. I was especially fond of one Ukrainian girl named Elena - a completely unique person, full of positivity and goodwill, fun, smart, incredibly loyal and filled with divine love for all God's creation. I am still totally in love with that girl, but back then we were so drawn towards each other that became almost inseparable. In those days I had one more special friend, more precisely, a friend of my entire adulthood - Nana. I had known Nana from the first year of university and we had been very close since then. She was the only Georgian in our surroundings, and that's because she moved from New York to New England to reside nearby us. Nana literally lived in the heart of Pentecostal community and they very faithfully took care of her during the entire time of her stay in America. In return, she taught their kids how to play the piano. Dimitri, Nana and I often had heated debates with our Pentecostal friends on a religious topic, but this did not hurt our friendship even a bit. Of course, they tried to save our souls by converting us to their faith, but in the end we all remained faithful to our own believes. Although those discussions might have seemed fruitless, but I'm sure they greatly helped both parties to become less radical and more tolerant of each other's religious feelings.

    As you see, our spiritual life had become much more diverse and richer in America, and this only strengthened the foundation of our faith. We were orthodox Christians and the Saint George's Cathedral and its great community remained the major influence on our everyday life. The dramatic shift in my career was also facilitated by the kindness of one of its parishioner's who I have already mentioned, Debby. In one of the early days of our acquaintance she asked me if I knew how to sew. I said that I did. Actually, I'm pretty good at it. So, in a few days or so she introduced me to her home designer, Janet who happened to have been looking for a seamstress at the time. Initially Janet took me on as a seamstress for a trail period of two weeks; by the end of the following month I was already promoted to the position of a work floor manager; in six months or so I became a decorator, and after three years of working at that place I realized that it was time to quit working for somebody else and start my own business. In the beginning everybody around me thought that I was making a huge mistake.

"Are you going mad?"They argued. "Who in his/her right mind quits a steady job with a good salary? 15 bucks an hour! Not every American has such an income. And who are you? A poor illegal without any rights or opportunities!"

Of course, all their arguments bore some seeds of truth, but I trusted my gut more and, as time proved it, I was right. Working as an independent designer turned out to be rather successful for me and I don't appraise it as only blind luck. A number of prerequisites contributed to this. First of all, I've got an inherent eye for beauty which no one can acquire unless it's bestowed upon you from above. The second prerequisite was a solid basic knowledge, especially in the fields of geometry and fine arts, and for that I thank the Soviet educational system which was superb during my student years. The third precondition - me being a typical workaholic – I deem as the 'must' requirement for any kind of accomplishment. And the last but not least raison d'être of my humble success was the economic situation in the United States itself.

Trade and industry were still booming back then. Most of my clients belonged to the upper middle class. They all ran small or medium size businesses, making plenty of money and then gladly investing it in the renovation of their homes. There were many other decorators/designers in our area but I never had any trouble finding clients. On the contrary, I was so loaded with orders that I hardly ever had time for anything else. My specialty in the design business primarily included making window treatments and bed accessories. I almost never worked with premade patterns and always preferred getting the challenging projects, such as dressing up two-storied living room or hall windows, upholstering the oddly shaped furniture, clothing walls with satin fabrics, beautifying fancy master bedrooms with sophisticated accessories, or transforming an ordinary kitchen into a nineteenth-century mid-west barn. Were your windows arched, round or hexagon shaped? No problem, I would calculate and make a pattern suitable just for them. Were they crooked or uneven for some reason? No worries. I would trick the eye and make them look perfectly fine. Sometimes I got really fun projects, like making someone's patio look like a wild forest, or adorning a fake fireplace with sitting pillows that looked like rocks. Reflecting the individuality of the customers in my work always gave me a special pleasure. Were they fun loving youngsters or introverts, simple folks or stylish fashion-mongers, I always kept their characters in mind while working on their projects.

Every now and again I used to collaborate with some other designers and house construction consultants. Such teamwork was always very beneficial for both sides. I particularly liked working with two ladies, Judy and Elizabeth as both were distinguished by a high level of professionalism and great, agreeable characters.

It's no surprise that with such an intense working schedule, I hardly ever had any time left for my family. I could relax and have a nice chat with my husband only during our regular early coffee hours at a nearby cafe called Panera Bread, in East Longmeadow.

Later, when my business grew and it required more people, I started hiring temporary seamstresses from time to time. As for Dimitri, he became responsible for all our installations. So what once started as a one woman's everyday job swiftly transformed into a family business. This change definitely had its pros and cons. One of the most important advantages of it was the pleasure of seeing my husband more frequently. Unfortunately, I couldn't say the same about our girls. I missed them all the time because they were always out, studying at school, or practicing field hockey with their teammates, or attending away games in one of the nearby cities. The typical fate of the typical teenagers' parents.

While reading these lines you probably fall under the false impression that our life was exactly the same as those of ordinary Americans'. Quite often even we were deceived by that erroneous illusion but, as a matter of fact, our reality was a far cry from that. Our lack of legal status was constantly loomed in front of us as soon as we dared to show even the simplest enterprising, even such a basic one as ordering fabrics for my projects, for example. I had to do all such operations by using other designers' accounts and, as you can guess, it always cost me a significant chunk of the profit. However, even under such unfavorable circumstances, I still managed to achieve some modest accomplishments. In 2007 several of my biggest projects appeared in the winter/spring issue of the prestigious design magazine, Living Spaces, and one of them even appeared on the front cover. The colorful pictures of luxurious patios, castle-like halls, and elegant master-bedrooms were also accompanied by two long articles presenting the readers with detailed information about those dream-houses and their owners. By and large, both articles were crediting the work of the amazingly talented home consultant, Elizabeth, who oversaw the whole constructions of those beautiful houses but my name was also mentioned in the articles as a designer/fabricator's and at that point in time I was quite satisfied even with such a modest achievement.

If I were asked, I would assess my career in the design field as a successful one, and many others around me, especially among my colleagues, shared the same opinion. This is why people were always baffled when I mentioned in private conversations that design was not my first priority and my heart truly belonged to another master, to writing. But heavens know that it was true. Otherwise I cannot explain the fact that during that period of my professional life, literally out of the blue, I'd suddenly become infected with the craziest idea of my life - to start working on a historical novel about the Persian Empire. And let me tell you in a few words how this madness began.

From my early childhood I had a small lump on my left hand. It never bothered me, and I never paid any attention to it. But in America, probably because of overusing the hand while working with fabrics and scissors, the lump started growing larger and became quite painful, so I decided to get rid of it. Eventually I had a surgery and couldn't work for a while. To tell you the truth, doing nothing is the worst thing that can ever happen to me. I became increasingly annoyed by all of the extra free time, which I considered rather more frustrating than relaxing. So, irritated by my frequent discontented sighs and incomprehensible grumbles, in order to restore peace and quiet at home somehow, Dimitri decided to take me and the kids to the movies. It was not so often that we did anything together as a family, so we all loved the idea.

We watched One Night with the King, a new blockbuster release which featured Persian King Xerxes and Jewish girl Esther's stirring love affair. But I felt quite disappointed by the movie and not because it was such a loose adaptation of one of the most popular biblical tale, but because it completely missed the most important factors of the historical genre: the proper sense of the period and a deep understanding of the particular culture. Although it was a pretty well made movie in the best traditions of Hollywood and was very pleasant to watch, I still couldn't catch even a tinge of Persian or, at least, Oriental spirit in it. It was a typical love story of our contemporary young couple, definitely from Europe or Northern America, who for some reason were dressed up in pseudo-Persian attire. Now, some of you may ask how I know that and why you should trust my opinion. Well, although we, Georgians, aren't Iranians, we are from the same region. For many centuries the mighty Persian Empire had been an archenemy of our tiny, Christian kingdom but fortunately, all that feuding and hostility is behind us. Nowadays we peacefully coexist and instead of the negative aspects of our past, both countries are more concentrated on the centuries-old, rich cultural relationship with each other. Based on this, I can safely say that although we, I mean the Georgians, are not similar to the Iranians in many ways, at least we can understand the peculiarity of their Oriental character and feel the depth of their ancient spirit.

Thus, provoked by the flamboyant Hollywood movie, I suddenly felt urge to write something short about Achaemenid Persia. My next step was very predictable – I swiftly ran to the nearest library and I'm so glad that I did, otherwise I may never have discovered the real treasure of American life – its magnificent libraries.

Cut a long story short, many things happened after that and a project that initially was intended as an in-one-fell-swooped tiny narrative gradually materialized into a massive multi-volume sequence of approximately 3 000 pages. This madness has already cost me twelve years of uphill struggle and the work is not completely done yet. But none of that would have ever happened if not for my preceding success in the design business which provided me with a relatively high income which, in its turn, gave me an opportunity to allocate at least eight-hour-of-everyday, ruthless labor to this project. That would never have happen if I hadn't come to America and polished my knowledge of the English language, which has given me access to immeasurably more sources of the latest scientific and archeological discoveries and research in the areas of my interests. And last but not least, I might never have found my true passion in life and my novel would never have had the chance to be delivered if not for the amazing American public library network in the development of which, as far as I know, the lion's share is attributed to Andrew Carnegie (also a former poor immigrant, by the way).

I am not going to further concentrate on my novel here because my literary work is not the topic of the present narrative. I'll only add one more thing – that the inability to travel back and forth to Georgia cost me quite a lot of trouble in dealing with the technical difficulties during the preparation for the publication of the first three volumes of my novel.

Chapter 7

Unfortunately, the lack of proper residential documents cost us way more damage when it came to our children. From the very beginning, as I'd imagine most parents would, we'd taken all possible precautions to keep the kids in the dark about our legal problems, and for a while we were quite successful in this. But as time passed it became more and more difficult to hide the truth from them. The kids simply couldn't understand our unreasonably overprotective behavior in situations which they deemed as absolutely harmless. Both our girls were brilliant students, with excellent marks and even better social attitudes, so teachers loved them and often rewarded them with all sorts of amazing opportunities such as visiting the White House in Washington DC or attending the conference of the future World leaders in Australia. Although all of those activities were fully sponsored by the state, we always kindly refused to let our kids participate. Everyone hated us for that: our children - because they thought that we were unjust and cruel and the teachers -probably for the same reason, or maybe they suspected that we were members of some weird religious sect or something like that. Anyway, whenever we politely denied the generous offers, it was hard not to notice the sincere surprise in the teachers' eyes, which was immediately followed by the distinctive spark of sharp indignation as they were trying to hide their fugitive glances.

It was really painful to endure all of the undeserved blame but over time the situation had gradually exacerbated and finally reached a point when Dimitri and I had no choice but unveil our secret to our daughters and ask them to keep it quiet. Nino was an eleventh grader then and Mariam – a freshman in the Springfield Central High school. The girls reacted absolutely differently to that shocking news.

"You've ruined my life!" –Nino burst out in anger.

"We had no choice. We could all die from starvation if we stayed in Georgia," – I tried to explain our actions.

"I'd prefer to be dead!"- She blurted out in response and dashed to her room.

Mariam's reaction was less dramatic. She actually didn't say a word and Dimitri and I felt relieved because of it; at least one of our kids was not completely overwhelmed by the news we thought, but pretty soon we found out how mistaken we were. In a very short time Mariam changed so much that not only us, but everybody around us were alarmed by it. Usually cheerful and lively, she became extremely introverted and inert all of a sudden. Even her appearance had significantly changed; in a few months she gained a lot of weight; but the worst consequences of her silent rebellion we reaped in her education. When I saw Mariam's following midterm school report, it was so unbelievably bad that at first I thought that some mistake must have been made. It indicated that the straight A student and ultimate teachers' pet, our daughter, nearly failed almost all of her classes. When I rushed to the school to find out what was going on, I learned to my horror that during the whole semester Mariam hadn't submitted even a single homework assignment. The teachers also complained about her lack of participation during class activities. She was just lying on her desk with her eyes closed throughout entire lessons and upon teachers' admonishments simply replied that she was not sleeping and could hear everything that the teacher was explaining perfectly well. Perhaps Mariam was telling the truth because she was still getting 100s for most of her tests; this is how she managed getting those miserable C-s and D-s. The teachers were very concerned about her alarming behavior and advised me to take her to the doctor's office as they suspected that there could be some medical reasons behind her sudden personality change. But I already knew what we were dealing with.

I had many conversations with Mariam after that, and I tried many different tactics to persuade her to reverse her attitude towards learning: I tried to convince her with gentle exhortation, I tried to win her over with compelling arguments, and I even tried to force her to submit by using parent's almighty weapon of enforcing restrictions but nothing really worked. Always remaining nice and polite, she still proved to be the most uncooperative person I have ever known. Her everlasting argument was always about the same, which I could summarize in these words: "Why should I delude myself with vain hopes when we both know that I have no future."

And don't you think that we had any break from Nino either. She was persuasively demanding her rights too. "I don't want to be illegal. End of story! Send me back home!" – That had become her ultimate motto for the rest of our stay in America.

Whether we liked it or not, we had to admit that the heavens had granted us with the world's most stubborn children. Thus after several months of fruitless battles, Dimitri and I had no choice but to give up and let Nino decide on her own fate. We only asked her to postpone her trip to Georgia till the summer. She would have finished the eleventh grade by then and I would have had time to find a suitable school for her back home.

We bought a ticket for Nino for August 10, 2008. Then we threw a beautiful farewell party for her in the best American tradition. All of her friends came to say goodbye to her. Many tears were shed, many wishes were spilled that bitter-sweet day but by the end everybody begged her to stay, not to leave. Fruitlessly, of course. After that evening it finally dawned on me that nothing could ever change my obstinate daughter's mind. But, as soon as I finally succumbed to an inescapable outcome, the heavens immediately proved to me that we know nothing about Fate.

Nino had to leave on August 10, and on August 8 the infamous five-day war broke out between Russia and Georgia. What can one call that if not fate? After that we didn't have to take any measures. The airline itself had canceled all flights to Tbilisi since its international airport was constantly being shelled. Those five days were the most agonizing for our family, especially for me. The city where my parents live is practically surrounded by the strategic objects that the aggressor's air force had been focusing on: the airport from one side and the military base from the other, so no surprise that I was dying from fear. A few times, when I was able to break through and reach my mom by phone, I could even hear the explosions from the bombing. It was terrifying. Dimitri and I immediately wanted to go back to Georgia. I don't know how our presence would have helped anyone over there but we wanted to be with our family anyway. After five days, thanks to the intervention of the international community, especially to the five presidents of European countries who braved to arrive in Tbilisi and by their physical presence, factually shielded our capital and its habitants from the bombing, and thanks to the American government who eagerly took up Senator McCain's fiery call: "Today we are all Georgians!" and sent the U.S. Sixth fleet aircraft carriers towards the Georgian ports, the Russian aggression was finally curbed. But even after that, the situation continued to be extremely dangerous for several months.

For Dimitri and me any talks about Nino's return to embattled Georgia were out of the question, although Nino herself still kept insisting that once things settle down she could fulfill her initial plans. But as many of you probably know, the Russian occupation of Georgian territories remains unsolved till the present.

Unfortunately, our tiny country was not the only one that got in trouble in those days. Everything around us felt as though the whole world had been contaminated by some kind of deadly fever. The U.S. economy was rapidly weakening too, plunging its population into great confusion and fear. Of course, all of those negative aspects had its significant impact on our life as well. Apart from that, we had other kinds of problems too. One of them was my husband's employment.

Although Dimitri's work could hardly be considered well paid one, it provided us with an excellent family health insurance, Blue Cross & Blue Shield, and how important this is for any average working class household, doesn't need further explanation. As a set up mechanic, he used to serve several carton cutting devices on the industrial line. All of the machinery at Milton Bradley was pretty old and tended to break down quite often. So Dimitri's task at Hasbro was not only physically extremely hard but it was emotionally very stressful as well since all other personnel's peace work-salary depended on the mechanic's performance. The conveyor line needed more than two set up mechanics, so many American guys had been employed during Dimitri's working period in Milton Bradley but none of them could stay for more than a couple of months at most. There was only one man, an old immigrant of Portuguese origin, who managed to stay at the same position for more than ten years. The second in line was Dimitri, who withstood more than five years. Towards the end, the working conditions for set up mechanics even further deteriorated. Milton Bradley started laying off its employees, partly due to the nation-wide recession, and also some rumors were circulating among employees that the company had been gradually moving offshore, to Mexico, so that could be another reason. The workload itself was not reduced and now Dimitri had to serve twice as many machines as before for the same salary, plus he had to work twelve hours a day and sometimes even weekends. Eventually, such intense labor had become absolutely unbearable for my poor, ailing husband who suffered from diabetes, and by the end of 2008, Dimitri had to quit his work at Hasbro. As a result, we had lost our steady income and the family health insurance with it. I was still loaded with lots of work but it could scarcely cover our living expenses. In addition, I had to buy health insurance, as Massachusetts's new law required one for all of its residents, and I had to support my parents back in Georgia as well, (Dimitri's mother had already passed away the previous year.).

Chapter 8

I think there are some special moments in everyone's life when providence clearly indicates to the person that the time for a big change has come. Like in Johnny Depp's famous movie "Chocolat." Remember that film? Every time when the North Wind blows, Vianne, the main protagonist of the story, unmistakably knows that it's not just an ordinary wind, but the spirit of her Mayan ancestors' whispering to her that it's time to leave the old, familiar place and get ready for new adventures. This is exactly how I felt that time.

But not only adverse circumstances forced us to leave the USA. After the Rose Revolution the criminal situation had greatly improved in Georgia. Although the unemployment rate remained sorely high, in terms of democratic development, our country was making gigantic paces. Our then-President Michael Saakashvili had also called his compatriots living abroad to come back and take an active part in the construction of new Georgia.

And finally, the last and the most important reason of our decision was that we all were sick and tired of being illegals. God is our witness that we never intended to become ones and what happened, only happened by virtue of circumstances beyond our control. But now the longer we remained in the swamp of illegality, the more responsible we felt about it. It was time to gain the courage and do the right thing.

But again, as soon as we had reached the verdict, another unbelievable obstacle emerged in our way. But this time, not a wicked calamity but human kindness itself must have decided to oppose our plans. Believe it or not, when our American friends learned about our decision to leave the USA, (and I must particularly emphasize here that most of them were conservative type individuals with strong anti-illegal immigration sentiments,), they launched a full scale Campaign against it. The members of Saint George's community were especially active in it. Of course, everybody was curious about what made us to come to such a sudden decision, and we named our economic hardship and lack of legal documents as the main reason for it. Hearing that, our friends protested loudly:

"It's not fair. You are hard-working, honest people, not some welfare seeking morons. You are exactly the type of immigrants America needs. You shouldn't leave. You belong here!"

Now, get ready for the most jaw dropping moment of our story, because only in fairy tales may you bump into such an unbelievable extravaganza. After discussing our situation among them, our friends came up with such a crazy plan that for a moment, Dimitri and I became speechless: they announced that they would cover all of our financial expenses until our immigration problems would finally be fixed. And they proposed this unprecedented offer in such a sincere and tender way that we had no choice but to gratefully accept it.

At the present, while we are asked by our Georgian countrymen about the USA and its people, we always recall this incredible episode as the most vivid manifestation of the uniqueness of American spirit. Unfortunately, most of our listeners simply do not believe us, assuming that we are just exaggerating events. But believe me, we are not! Our American friends really rented for us a new apartment, a smaller one but very cozy and with a better location. They also took care of all our utility bills for almost a year. Now, if you add to it a car, which was personally presented to me with the intention of restoring gender equality in our family (which was never breached, by the way,), a brand new washing machine and a dryer, most of our furniture, and a countless number of smaller gifts that we had received during the previous years, you must agree that there is hardly any place left for any kind of exaggeration here.

But even all this incredible generosity from our friends could not bring us peace of mind because we were not the type of people who could misuse anybody's kindness for too long, especially when we did not see any hope that our immigration dilemma would be soon resolved. Therefore, after a while, we again decided to leave, this time for good. Our friends took the news very badly. Some of them hardly talked to us after that anymore, as if we betrayed their loyalty, or didn't appreciate their generosity or who knows what else. None of those assumptions were true of course; we simply decided to do what felt right.

That was difficult time for our family. The only thing that sincerely pleased me then was the sweet foretaste of the nearing reunion with my parents but even such a seemingly sure thing was not destined to become true; in that spring my mom died of cancer. I lost my Madonna. I was never told how far her illness had progressed, so the news struck me like lightning from the blue. My mom's blazing gaze, fevered by abysmal hopelessness, while seeing us off at the Tbilisi airport on the day of our departure immediately flashed before my eyes, and her soundless whisper: "I'll never see you again", reverberated in my ears. That was my last straw. I knew we had to go home without any delay, but we still faced one unsolved dilemma. This time it concerned our older daughter.

Nino was finishing high school that year and we hoped that she would continue her education in one of the English-language universities in Tbilisi, but, as it turned out, the school enrollment laws had changed there since we left the country. Before, every university had its own admission regulations but now, in order to enroll in any university, all applicants who were Georgian citizens had to pass The United National Examinations, and do it in Georgian language. This change itself was quite a progressive step in the improvement of the education system in Georgia, where corruption was rampant in the past, but personally for us, it meant one more obstacle we had to overcome; for American high school graduate, Nino, there was no chance of passing the exams in Georgian, not in the next few years at least. Although, one small loophole still remained in that difficult situation. Georgian universities welcomed transfer students from any American college, so Nino could enroll in a college in the U.S. and transfer to the Georgian one later. But this plan also had one huge disadvantage: by that time Nino would have been 18, which meant she would automatically have become illegal, exactly the outcome she was trying so hard to escape. As you see, no matter what we would do, Nino would be still losing, one way or another, but we had to come up with a decision anyway. In the end we agreed to leave Nino with one of her friends, whose parents kindly promised us to look after her like after their own child. For now we were busy preparing for the nearing departure. But in the meantime, perhaps we had forgotten that sudden surprises have no limits, so we were once again reminded.

As you already know, nine years earlier we had adopted a dog, named Onyx. In seven years after that another four-legged creature, a yellow kitten named Lawrence had blessed us with his arrival. None of us had even invited this rascal. He had just laid his cunning eye on our domain and conquered it by force. Sure, we adopted that purring little cuteness; not a very wise move from our side but that was nothing compare to our third, completely reckless step which made it official that everyone in our family was a bit crazy. Literally during the last days of our stay in the U.S. Nino brought us the most beautiful feline I have ever seen, Joachim. Disguised in glamorous silver fur and with evil-looking, emerald eyes, this nine year-old Norwegian forest cat weighted only about eight pounds but could scare anyone to near death, and not without a reason. With his razor-sharp, thin claws he could easily cut any offender into small strips in the blink of an eye, a magic trick he had apparently overused to his own dismay. We learned from Nino that Joachim's previous owners had brought two new kittens to their house and had decided to euthanize the rebellious old one. I was shocked, as was Dimitri but what could we do?

"Mom, if we don't help him, they'll put him asleep!" Nino begged.

"But how? We're leaving in few weeks."

"So what? At least these few weeks he'll be alive."

Once again emotions shamefully beat our common sense, and Joachim stayed.

It was really difficult for the old cat to adapt to a new environment. For three days he sheltered himself under the dirty bathtub, and then he sneaked into Mariam's room and hid under her bed for some more days. At about the same time he started accepting food but not us, not until one night, when a strange feeling of pressure awoke Mariam. It was Joachim cautiously hovering over her chest. That was the turning point in our relationship; the ice was broken and one by one, he accepted all of us and even allowed us to stroke his head. The next big step for Joachim was to find common ground with our other pets. For the belligerent old fighter, gullible little Lawrence was no problem at all but Onyx was another story. You should have seen how quietly, without any extra movement, Joachim sneaked past the sleeping dog for the very first time. We almost cried while witnessing how bravely the battered old cat was fighting his inborn instincts and finally defeated the fear.

That was it! If the cat found the courage within himself to rise above human disloyalty and to accept our family with all of its furry members, how could we betray him for the second time and break his tiny heart? The outcome of this was obvious: Joachim was coming with us to Georgia - the decision which was easy to proclaim but hard to fulfill.

When my brother heard about it, he snarled at me over the phone:

"What? Two cats and a dog?! Stop saying nonsense! Better bring a car! Even used cars are very expensive here. So, everybody who has a chance is bringing a car from America or from Germany."

Believe it or not even my father was doubtful about our decision.

"Our flat is too small for them, my dear. Take the dog and leave the cats there. Believe me, it's better for them to stay there," – he advised softly.

In short, everyone in Georgia was against our intentions, and most of our American friends totally agreed with them.

"Besides, it's stupid, you don't have money for that! Have you got any idea how much it will cost you?"

And they were all right; we didn't have any extra savings at all. Actually I had to work days and nights non-stop for the last few months to collect enough money to buy three air tickets and to leave the rest of the sum to Nino to pay for the first semester of college. Not surprisingly, all that hardship stressed us out quite a bit, but the very last minute a sudden windfall proved it again that none of our little troubles can escape from the eyes of the Almighty God and thus, we must never fall into despair. We had one special friend, Mark by name. He lived in Longmeadow, the city of the local affluent, and we knew that for some time now he was thinking of refreshing his home. So, when Mark learned that we were leaving soon, he asked Dimitri to do some painting for him and as a payment, he offered to buy plane tickets for us. Of course, we gladly seized this opportunity, although it was quite hard to squeeze a new big order into our already tight schedule. But, as it turned out, it was just an elegant ploy on Mark' part. In reality he didn't need any immediate renovations; he just wanted to help us out.

What do you say to that? If you remember we had come to America thanks to a fluke and now we were leaving in exactly the same manner. But do you believe in the fortuitousness of such coincidences? Because I don't.

In a word, we got our tickets, plus some extra money on our hands. Of course we didn't buy any car. Instead we purchased three special pet tickets and air-travel-approved cages for our furry gang. After that, we went through all the necessary procedures required by law for taking pets abroad, such as getting every imaginable vaccination for them, chipping them in case they were lost, and getting special travel documents for them. Believe it or not, our four-legged companions needed as much paperwork as we did, if not even more. In some sense, this whole routine around our pets turned out to be rather helpful for me personally. The thing is, I was so worried that at the very last minute U.S. Customs might not allow us to take our beloved pets with us that I almost forgot about our own legal problems. Thankfully, our departure was not marked by any further complications except one curious case which I'm about to tell you.

Now, you all probably know that travelling with pets by plane is not a laughing matter; it's regulated by various strict rules, and not all of them are particularly fair-minded ones, I must say. I'll give you a quick example. Our gentle sweethearts, Onyx and Lawrence, as they were heavy guys, were sentenced to the cargo section, but our evil genius, Joachim, thanks to his tiny weight, was allowed to come with us into the cabin. So I put his cage on my lap and tried to soothe him as he was constantly hovering inside. After a while he seemed to calm down a bit and I relocated his cage under my feet as I was tired myself and needed some peace and quiet. You know how it is during the flight; of course I dozed. But what kind of evil genius would Joachim be if he didn't punish such negligence. I don't know how much time had passed before a weird feeling of uneasiness woke me. When I opened my eyes, everything was calm and tranquil around. The lights were switched off and passengers were slumbering in their chairs. I sighed in relief and was about to nod off again but I wanted to pet my little devil first, so I slipped my hand under my feet and froze in horror; the cage was empty. I immediately woke Dimitri and Mariam.

"He sneaked out!"

"What?! Who?!"

"Joachim!"

Without any further questions they both got up and quietly tiptoed down the aisles, checking under every passenger's seat. I remained in my place, trying to figure out what to do if they failed to find our fugitive. Dimitri and Mariam were searching very carefully but some of the passengers still woke up and asked them what they were looking for. After they learned what was the matter, most of the passengers responded to our problem with understanding, except for one old lady who suddenly panicked:

"Oh, my Goodness! Are you telling me the truth? A cat, not a snake?!"

"No, ma'am, it's just a tiny cat," Dimitri tried to calm her down but his soothing whisper couldn't convince the lady, so it became necessary to call the flight attendants. Of course I joined the group.

I was quite scared because I thought that all this fuss might draw potentially risky attention to us and our 'illegality' could be revealed. Next, they would question if we even had a right to take our pets with us from America and all three of them would be taken from us. Today I understand that I was quite exaggerating a pretty ordinary situation then but as they say, fear has big eyes and I was totally overwhelmed by it. Fortunately not everybody contemplates the world through the prism of the poor illegal's fevered imagination, so to my big surprise and even bigger relief the crew members took the news as if dealing with runaway cats was their every day drudgery.

"Look around more carefully and you may find him," one of them advised us, rather unemotionally.

Doubtfulness behind those words alarmed me greatly and although I absolutely dreaded to further aggravate our situation, I couldn't refrain from asking:

"Is it possible that we don't?"

"If he sneaked into the machine section..." The young man didn't finish his sentence but the expression on his face said it all.

As the drowning man I clutched at our last straw:

"We will search the machine section after we land, right?"

But the pragmatic flight attendant coldly demolished all my hopes:

"I doubt it. Most likely the plane is scheduled to fly somewhere else pretty soon after landing, so there will be no time for that."

Now seriously frightened, Dimitri, Mariam, and I all vigorously renewed our search. Some passengers also volunteered to help us. There was no need to be very quiet anymore as pretty much everybody onboard was already awake and knew what was going on. Quite soon someone spotted our fugitive under the seat and the sneaky cat was returned to his hated cage. We sighed in relief, but the real sense of liberation came to me only a few hours later, at the very moment when my foot touched the ground of the Tbilisi airport, and I know why: we were not illegals anymore.

Chapter 9

More than eight years have passed after that day and many things have changed in our lives. Nino, instead of coming home to continue her education, as we had previously planned, got married and had a lovely church wedding which we, of course, couldn't attend. A severe retribution for our illegal past! Dimitri was particularly upset by the situation. Two weeks before the wedding, he suffered an extensive stroke. I do not claim that it happened solely because of our sorry circumstances but acute worries about our daughter's wedding certainly provoked that massive blow. We did not tell Nino about her father's illness; we did not want to overshadow her big day. She was so happy then... As for her education, since our son-in-law was a military man and Nino was following him everywhere wherever the army sent him, this issue was postponed for an indefinite period. Unfortunately, this marriage didn't work out well, mainly because of the army lifestyle, I guess, and after four years of marriage they finally divorced. Meanwhile, Nino has gotten into a new relationship and she is blessed with her first child, our precious Sophia Annette. And again, of course, I dearly wished to be with my daughter at such a crucial moment in her life, but I did not even think of applying to the embassy for a visa, knowing that the law does not have any human sentiments and hardly ever gives you any break.

And what are we doing now in Georgia? After returning home, Dimitri's health deteriorated even more. As I've mentioned above, in 2011 he suffered a major stroke and after many complications including a kidney failure he passed away in 2014. My friend Nana returned to Georgia in the fall of 2016, only to live in her homeland for a couple of weeks and die from cancer. Our beloved pets, Onyx and Joachim have also died of old age, taking a bit of our souls with them to heaven, (both were 14), and now only our yellow cat, Lawrence, stays with us as the lone relic of our American saga.

As for Mariam, she leads quite a busy life. She studied journalism at the American University in Bulgaria for three semesters but didn't complete it. At various times she has worked at the local historical museum and also taught English at the Academy of World Languages in Rustavi. At present she works as an English-speaking consultant for the Georgian Service Group that sells all kinds of pet supplies all over the European Union. No surprise that as a New England-bred girl, she is a women's rights militant advocate and also involved in many social projects, especially in monument protection issues. Thanks to her activities she travels a lot abroad. She has visited the UK as a Georgia's representative in the International Public Speaking Competition held in London. Mariam also had a couple of opportunities to visit the USA - once when she was chosen as a staff member of the Georgian delegation of the National Model United Nations Conference in New York City, and the second time when American Rotary Club invited her as their translator during the visit of the Georgian delegation of disabled children's parents to the USA, but both times she was denied a visa by the American Embassy, and you can easily guess why. How fair it is to block the career development of a young prospective girl who voluntarily left America in order not to stay there illegally, and what kind of message does such a state policy send to other young illegal immigrants who may be considering the possibility of returning to their countries, I leave for your consideration.

For my part, Dimitri's illness and following death nearly killed me too, but I survived. Now I'm on the road to recovery, working 24/7 as usual, teaching English to local students as a freelance tutor, translating for various organizations, running an NGO for Women's Rights which I founded in 2014, and finishing the last volume of my novel about the Persian Empire in between. For a while I worked as an Ambassador's personal referent and Head of the Chancellery at the Embassy of Turkmenistan in Georgia but quickly became convinced that for a freethinker like myself no prestigious work or solid salary would outweigh the bliss of independence and quickly returned to the world of free enterprise. Clearly an influence of our American past.

In many respects, our living conditions have greatly improved. All our family: my dad, Mariam and I, along with our yellow American cat Lawrence and the newest member of our family, four-year-old black Labrador Alfie, live in a small cozy house conveniently located on the top of a hill in the very heart of the old part of the capital city. Two years ago, while looking for a new dwelling place, I chose this particular house among many other options mainly because of its marvelous panoramic view. From its dining room windows and the open-air veranda all Tbilisi lies as if on the palm of your hand. The view becomes especially charming at night, when the city, swallowed by the darkness, starts to flicker as millions of fireflies at your foot. On the opposite end of the city, also on a hill, at about our level, or maybe a little higher, the famous cylinders of the local billionaire, Bidzina Ivanishvili, glisten. He, too, is looking down at the city, from a different angle, of course, and with the eyes of a billionaire, from a distance in which everything below, even the slums, seems perfect. I jokingly call myself a mini-Ivanishvili, as I admire the city almost as he does. On this our resemblance to the local tycoon unfortunately ends, since financially we are still far from the level of the American middle class, never mind the rich.

Meanwhile, life is quite expensive in Tbilisi, but since Mariam and I both earn relatively well, we quietly cope with all the expenses and even manage to put some money aside. I must admit that we both are crazy about traveling and most of our savings are spent on it. Georgia is one of the popular low and medium-budget tourist destinations for visitors from all over the world. Consequently, trips from here to other countries are also relatively cheap. Therefore, we can allow ourselves to visit different sights of the world once or twice a year. Almost every summer we enjoy our two-week vacation in Greece where we have close relatives from my father's side. We also travel to other countries for cultural enlightenment. We have already visited Turkey, Egypt, Bulgaria, Italy, and England and with God's help, we hope to continue our travels in future. To tell you the truth, I don't think that we could afford this kind of lifestyle if we stayed in America. Who would have thought n the distant 1999, when we ventured to seek temporary refuge in America that almost two decades later foreign aliens would start looking for a better life here, in Georgia. But truth is that more and more Americans, along with other westerners, are settling in Georgia probably because of extra comfort with minimal costs. Simplified business regulations and immigrant-friendly atmosphere also attract many foreigners. Even our family sheltered one such a trailblazer, an African-American guy, Kyle by name, for almost three months during last summer.

If I were asked what I feel about America today, I would certainly answer: The tremendous gratitude! After all, it's like a second motherland to me - the country that helped us to escape the most difficult years of the post-Soviet Georgia, the country that has raised our daughters into strong, independent young women, the country that laid the foundation of our present-day achievements by providing me with the main source of our income, fluency in English, and by giving me the boldness to become a non-native English writer.

If only you knew how I miss New England with its incredibly colorful autumn and its flickering white Christmas, our quick breakfasts at Panera Bread, where Dima and I frequently used to start our overloaded mornings, but most of all I miss our dearest friends who have left such deep traces in my memory.

Do I want to go to America again? Of course, I do. After all, I've got my first-born child and her precious daughter there. I don't know what the future will bring to our family. Will I ever hug my Nino again, see my grandchild, and take my part in her upbringing? Will I meet my son-in-law, John, in person? Will our family ever be reunited again and function as a normal one? Or am I, too, destined to share the fate of my mother and my husband and die with a broken heart? I can only pray that it is not my fate. Meanwhile, I'm waiting for those presumable ten years of banning to pass and then will try to get a new entry permit, although the lapse of a 10-year ban does not necessarily guarantee the end of the trouble. Remember? Technically the ban did not even apply to Mariam, since she was a minor during her stay in America, but she was still denied the right to re-enter the country. But despite all these discouraging facts, my oldest daughter, Nino, still remains optimistic and keeps saying that everything is going to be all right. She even incites me, wishing that I have already applied for a visa. I understand her Impatience: after all, right now, while with a little baby, she needs mom's help the most.

Well, that's the end of our story, and, now as a closing remark, I'd like to add a few final words. We, humans, are like water, and water squeezed by the elements will always seek a breach. So instead of cursing the water, why don't just fix the breach. But while doing so one must always remember why God has granted the mankind the glorious Year of Jubilee.

The End

Other books by Tsira Gelen

And God Requireth That which is Past

The Invincible Empire

Chapter 1

Nativity

A quiet stillness settled over the semi-darkened hall. Only the impatient pacing of the burly middle-aged man disturbed the total silence. From time to time he glanced uneasily at the dark winding wooden stairs from beneath his creased brow. The man's deeply wrinkled forehead crumpled even further and he clenched his teeth so tightly that the already thin lips under his graying beard were scarcely visible. The creak of a door echoed nearby. He listened. Somebody was climbing the stairs leading from the yard to the kitchen. The man looked in that direction. He was unable to see what was happening behind the old oak door, but he could hear it.

"Khongul, have you told the boy to bring firewood?" a woman's voice demanded.

"Yes, he will bring it," the man mumbled back.

Then footsteps rang toward the hall which were followed once more by the creaking of a door and a worn, hardened man donning a sheep skin vest walked in. The strong scent of smoke and burning dried dung wafted in with him. It was apparent that he had come directly from his flock.

"Any news yet, Saurmag?"

"No, Khongul, nothing yet."

The newly arrived man sank down next to the mahvsh's armchair and started playing with his felt hat. The final days of the short mountain summer were coming to an end. Normally, Khongul would have been with his herd at this time, getting the sheep from the summer pasture to the lowlands, but he was the host's cousin and he considered it his responsibility to be with him in his time of need. And this was quite a difficult time for the Svan chief, Saurmag indeed. His young wife had been struggling with labor pains for three days now, and still couldn't deliver. The Mahvsh's family tower was seized by such tension, as if an invisible enemy had come to the Svan valley and the inhabitants of these moss covered walls were awaiting a messenger from the battle field any minute now.

Outside it was bright and clear, but inside it was still rather dark. This was no surprise. The Svans built their towers so that these forebodingly elevated stone giants would serve as living quarters as well as fortresses. The middle level was where the family's main hall was situated, which was separated from the kitchen by a solid wall, thought the remaining three walls were built with such narrow peeping slits that a warrior would barely be able to fit one shoulder through to shoot an arrow at his enemy.

The scarce light that drifted in from outside stretched in straight lines on the bumpy old floor, lighting only a small portion of the hall. The rest of the place was covered in a shady haze. The only way into this formidable tower was up the wooden ladder coming down from the kitchen, but during times of war, even that would be pulled up or burned and the only door, now hanging at an unreachable height, would be barred from the inside. Then the Svan's peaceful home would truly become an impenetrable fortress.

If I don't do something about this floor someone will undoubtedly break a leg. Khongul peered into the hole in front of him as he knelt to tie up the loose straps of his leather shoes, but he couldn't make anything out in the dark crack. The huge store room beneath the hall and kitchen had no doors or windows at all. One could only get there through the little entrance in the floor of the kitchen. At the moment the place was empty, but during heavy snows, the chief's family would keep their small livestock in this storage for months. This was why the warm, homey smell of sheep, hay, and manure would still be strong even in the late summer.

Khongul quit inspecting the crack and looked about in order to entertain himself in the silence. His wife, Darsia hadn't lit the lanterns; only one torch was fastened at the top of the winding stairs. The man knew that they had a full supply of oil and Persian radanake in the tower, but the thrifty woman was saving this fuel, bought from Babylonian merchants at the price of blood, for the cold winter days.

What a stingy woman. She couldn't even light the Mahvsh's hearth at such a special time? the man thought and glanced toward the winding stairs again.

Upstairs was Saurmag's tiny bedroom, as well as a spacious room for his daughters. The Chief's sons, along with the guards slept right there, in the main hall. Piles of flattened hay, covered with felt cloaks were still scattered about in every corner. If he didn't count the Mahvsh's heavy Oaken armchair, one long, low dining table against the wall, and the stool on which he sat himself as too much comfort, there were only two large wooden chests in the room to hold weapons and nothing else. A Svan man needed no other belongings. The clothes he had, he wore on his back, as for food, the buzzing women in the kitchen would worry about that. However, little scraps, knittings, and jewelry, all dear to the women's hearts, were kept in the girls' chamber.

Khongul was brought back from his thoughts by his cousin's heavy sigh.

"Don't worry, brother, my wife here tells me this happens a lot down in the valley. It will be a little hard for the lady at first, but it will turn out alright."

Saurmag glanced thankfully over at his reassuring friend. The Svan chief was a brave man. He had proved his right to being the lord of the mountains in endless battles by shedding blood and sweat, but now fear had crept into his hard gaze.

Dressed in dark, dull colors, there wasn't much that set the chief apart from the other valley folk. Saurmag's clothes spoke for that fact that he wasn't wealthy, but no one could say he was poor either. Over his patched up, canvas shirt and worn leather pants, the chief wore a sleeveless, colorful wool vest that his first wife had woven for him which was fastened at his waist by a wide leather belt. He wore nothing on his head, and kept his graying hair and thick beard short. Still, one thing stood out from his modest attire. Saurmag's legs were covered by high necked pig skin boots. No one had seen such a wonder in the mountains yet. The chief had acquired it from a Parthian merchant during his visit to the lowlands and brought a pair exactly like his for Khongul as well. His cousin had been so thrilled by this foreign gift that he knelt to the ground and untied his straps to try them on right away.

"Khongul, brother, the merchant warned me to wrap my feet before putting them on."

"Yeah, right... they're not shoes that Khonchua's made." Khongul pulled the boots over his calloused feet.

He regretted his own negligence that very day. By evening, when the hobbling, stubborn man took his gift off, his feet were covered in bloody injuries and blisters. Never mind the boots, he had a hard time putting on even his own worn out shoes for days after. *Ah, what good can you expect from those damned lowlands!* The mountaineer concluded and never looked to his shiny boots, tossed in the corner, ever again.

No one knows for sure when the Svans first settled in the formidable Caucasian mountain range. Only one thing can be said for sure, it was maddening demands of the Kolchis kings that drove this independent tribe to the domain of Amiran, the mythical hero, who was chained by angry gods to the steep slopes of the double headed Elbrus for giving fire to mankind. Here, in the high mountains, every clan was equal. Every family lived in their own inaccessible towers. Each clan had their own head, the white bearded wise mahvsh, and the entire mountain was ruled by the Council of Elders. From the valleys to the mountain tops, the Mahvshs reined all. The chief, who was the head of the army, was also chosen by them.

Instead of trying to chase the Svans down their mountains in vain, the wise Kolchis kings decided to remain friendly neighbors.

Although Svans were not dependent on anyone, they would fight on their kin Kolchian tribes' side. A Svan always fought: fought in the mountains, fought in the valleys. He was a defender against their impudent northern neighbors' attacks, he wouldn't hesitate to raid the neighboring Sarmathian and Zykhian lands either; he defended Kolchis' northern borders; if needed, he would go as far south as to Moschi and Trapezos. A Svan knew no boundaries. For his country and honor, he would lay down his life without a second thought. One could say the only reason for a Svan's existence was to fight.

A proud mountaineer knew love as much as hate, valued hostility and friendship equally. He respected his family and loved his woman passionately. Once married, a Svan man would never look aside, he would never speak to another's wife, nor would he allow a single disrespectful glance toward a female family member go without bloodshed. A man would never cheat on his wife nor divorce her. Only in the case of death could he remarry, and even this was rare. The loyalty of a Svan father or a husband went beyond the human realm of understanding.

By strength, a woman did not fall short of a man. Hardened by the thin mountain air and harsh labor, a Svan woman, by stamina and endurance, could probably beat out any lowlander. A woman gave birth, took care of her family, wove thread and knitted. Occasionally, if the father of the family was away at war, she hunted and herded as well. If widowed, she would take the burden of both the man and the woman on her capable shoulders. The village took care of the orphans. When an enemy, knowing the men were away at war, raided a Svan village to steal the livestock (Who would even consider kidnapping a Svan woman!), the women would take up their swords and often times chase them away.

Assailed by the harsh winds and even harsher living conditions, one couldn't blame beauty on a Svan woman, but there was nothing more cherished than her in the mountains. A Svan man rarely ever married a lowlander beauty and only if he was madly in love. The villages never approved of these marriages. They knew from experience, in such families, the woman would suffer as would the man. A pretty, delicate woman would not last long in the mountain life.

A year ago, Saurmag committed just such a crime: he fell in love with a beautiful lowlander.

Last summer the Kolchis king sent rich gifts to the Svan chief and asked for a favor. This was the deal: The impudent Zykhians continued to pillage the valley Svans and Apshils, living near the northern border. They didn't spare the Greeks either. The last insult went so far that they even reached Dioscurias. The king sent his troops from Aia and Phasis but when they arrived, there was no sign of the assailants.

As usual, the Svans took the attack on their Kolchis counterparts as a personal insult and immediately gathered an army. Saurmag assigned his spies to every village in northern Kolchis, while he himself camped in a hidden valley. This tactic worked.

The Zykhians, bold from their previous successes, soon appeared in Kolchis. The chief let them go in deeper and deeper, then cut them off to the north and on a narrow path near the Greek city Pityos, he massacred them all. Then, the blood drunken Svans crossed the border and raided the enemy's nearby villages. During this raid, they landed a lot of spoils, including a rich caravan among them. They freed the merchants at the Greek city Naessos.

"Your precious lives for your useless goods!" the chief mocked the foreign merchants.

Saurmag freed all the caravan slaves without any cost. Slavery was unacceptable to the freedom loving Svans. They must either kill or release their enemy, there was no other way, but they rarely ever spared them.

Among the caravan slaves there were a few beauties. Hoping for big profit, the merchants had them well taken care of. They planned to take them to Persia for sale, but they never made it. Except for one, Saurmag left these beautiful women in the charge of his distant relative. The chief knew that such pretty girls wouldn't burden their kind host for long. The beauty worshiping Kolchian Zans would surely kidnap the lovely foreign girls.

One such maiden captured even Saurmag's heart. To be exact, it was she, the green eyed, flame haired young lady who had set her eyes on the formidable mountain chief first. The poor frightened captive shied away from everyone except the Svan chief, as if expecting protection only from him.

The young woman's behavior melted Saurmag's heart. It had been three years since the chief had become a widower. His family didn't burden the father of two daughters and seven sons, even the death of his wife changed little to nothing in his life. The children just sprang up on their own like mushrooms. Khongul's wife, Darsia took care of his home. Everything remained as it always did: Saurmag battled endlessly, and the house sat, forever waiting for his return.

To this day the chief hadn't even considered remarrying. Now everything was different. Suddenly Saurmag discovered that all these years he had been lusting for the warmth and love of a woman. A single shy glance from the green eyed foreigner aroused almost forgotten desires. Saurmag reached a decision: the Svan chief would marry the lowlander maiden.

The wedding was held that very summer. They had many guests from the mountains as well as the valleys. Even the Kolchis' king sent his oldest son, Prince Amiran, on behalf of Aia to honor the Svans.

Saurmag, tired of pacing, took a seat in his deceased father's chair. Closing his eyes, he submerged himself in old memories. Khongul secretly took a peek at the chief, wondering what was hidden behind his wrinkled forehead. At times, Saurmag would smile quietly; at times he furrowed his brows.

Over the past year many things happened, worthy of recollection. His wedding night protruded from a sea of memories. How he tiptoed to the heavy wooden door of their bedchamber, knowing that, she, his beautiful young bride was ready, waiting for him. Although heavily drunk, the bridegroom still couldn't calm his thrashing heart. Mustering his courage, he pushed the heavy door aside and entered the room…

Memories of that night still made him blush. The next morning, the exhausted yet cheerful groom left the room and bounded down the stairs, feeling young again. Many of the guests sat around the table of the wedding feast, still celebrating. A little distance from the table, The women were boiling lamb and its innards in a pot set on three legs. Only two paces from them, a ram was roasting whole on a spit. Beside the scorching clay plates, bakers, brought up from the lowlands, were bustling around. Young boys and girls were hurrying the already cooked food to the table on large trays. Saurmag's oldest sons kept up the steady supply of wine for their guests themselves. The smell of wine and excitement still hung in the morning air.

"Here's our groom!" thundered the Tamada upon seeing the chief, dressed in red and white attire with a cross-embroidered felt hat.

Everyone sprang to their feet, congratulating him once more, hugging him, blessing him.

"Saurmag my Lord, look what we've come to! Here we are, in Svaneti, so many drunken fellows, and lo: no swords have been drawn, no blood has been shed!" the overjoyed chief of the lowlander Svans smiled naughtily.

"Hey! Who said no blood has been shed? It has, I know it for sure!" the Zan chief sprang to his feet like a forest imp.

With his hand on his silver sword, the flushed mountaineer didn't know where to avert his eyes. The whole table was shaking with laughter.

That day Saurmag couldn't even look toward the women's quarters. When evening fell, the guests dispersed at last. The host finally managed to reach what he most desired. Standing in front of the bedchamber, the chief smiled to himself shyly. Just as he reached for the door, it sprang open on its own and Darsia towered over him. Saurmag froze in surprise. The woman shoved the baffled man, making him stumble back.

"Where do you think you're going?" Khongul's wife glared threateningly. "What, do you think, you're some kind of wolf and this poor woman your prey? Now, get out of here, and don't show your face till you're called!"

The bewildered chief went down to the hall and stopped in the middle of the room, dazed. Khongul's shadow moved from the wall. Wordlessly, he took his cousin's hand and like a child, drew him away.

Saurmag was only called to that tower two weeks later...

A woman's voice brought the Svan chief back to the present.

"Darsia, Darsia, bring water! Quickly!" At the top of the winding stairs, the midwife's tiny form darted into sight and immediately disappeared.

Both men sprang to their feet. Darsia rushed from the kitchen with an old faded cloth tying her damp hair back.

"Khongul, help me bring up the water! Hurry, hurry!"

The alarmed Svan hastily followed his wife. Soon they both reemerged. Khongul was carrying a boiling pot of water. Darsia hurried after him with a smaller cold one.

"Let me help you, brother," the chief extended his hands.

"No, no!" his cousin called, already darting up the stairs.

Saurmag started to pace again restlessly. Shortly Khongul joined him.

"How is everything?" the chief asked anxiously.

"How should I know? They wouldn't let me in." Khongul responded honestly, but seeing his friend's disappointment, added: "Well, since they asked for water, it should be soon now, Saurmag. It's always like this. The midwife's there, so is Darsia and the girls are helping too. Don't worry, brother, who hasn't given birth to a babe!"

No living thing on this earth had ever scared the Svan chief. Saurmag had looked death in the eye many times before and never even flinched. The loss of his first wife pierced the heart of the fearless chief. Distress, anger, helplessness, pain, they all took turns on him. But it was not fear.

This day, Saurmag felt something he never felt before. This new feeling crept into the body of the invincible Svan, and gnawed at him from the inside. Khongul was right, fear emanated from his eyes.

Soon the entire tower was filled with scurrying woman. The red and green high stockings of the girls, constantly running up and down the stairs, whirled past right before the two cousins' eyes. Then all went quiet, silence hung in the air. From time to time only a woman's screams rang through the still rooms. Soon this stopped too. The quiet weighed heavily on Saurmag's shoulders. Suddenly the cry of a child rang through the air, bringing everything back to life.

The men felt immediate relief. The chief headed for the stairs, but his cousin pulled him back.

"No Saurmag, don't. They will call you when it's time."

Time went by. Saurmag sat at the edge of the armchair. He couldn't understand why they hadn't called him yet.

"Do you think they forgot us?" Saurmag looked at his friend, puzzled.

"How could that be, my Lord? You know women. They're probably prettying up the mother and her babe to meet the father."

Finally, Darsia appeared at the top of the stairs. She motioned Saurmag to follow and disappeared. Saurmag took the stairs three at a time and approached the bedchamber. Darsia was already waiting for him. Head bowed, the woman led him in.

Chilling silence stirred in the grey room. Here, even the clear mountain air seemed to be wrapped in a dismal shroud. The only bright spot in the room was the fiery red locks scattered over the bed. Only the newborn's quiet breathing could be heard.

The familiar, nauseating smell of blood hit Saurmag hard upon entering the room. The father didn't even look in the baby's direction. Moving past the spinning wheel set in the center of the room, he headed straight for the bed, kneeled next to his wife and cautiously took her withered hand. The woman didn't move. A faint smile was frozen on her pale face as if glad to be free of all earthly matters.

"Sorry, my Lord. We did all we could. The poor thing was drained of blood," the midwife's trembling voice cried as she wiped her toothless mouth.

Darsia shot a quick angry glance at the old woman making her cease. Then Khongul's wife motioned something at the chief's eldest daughter standing by the wall. The girl approached her father, holding the newborn out for him. The chief didn't move.

"There will be time to grieve, Saurmag, for now the child needs to be taken care of." Darsia encouraged the chief.

"You know better than I, what to do." the devastated father looked away.

The chief's Daughter obediently drew back, but one glance from Darsia made her freeze. The Svan woman rested a hand on the kneeling man's shoulder and spoke in an unusually soothing voice.

"Where to find a nanny and how to take care of her, is of course on me, Saurmag. That's not what I'm talking about. You've lost your wife, she - her mother. Don't leave this little girl without a father's love as well. Hold her!"

His eldest daughter held out the newborn once more. The father looked down at his child with empty eyes. Tossing discontentedly in her older sister's arms, the little girl, with fuzzy red tufts of hair, was glaring about blindly with her emerald eyes.

Just like her poor mother. Struck by the similarities, Saurmag unconsciously reached for the child and carefully clutched her to his chest. Apparently the child felt the closeness of her parent. The little one yawned sweetly and started suckling on her fingers. Tears rolled down Saurmag's tan cheeks. Darsia motioned to the onlookers. They all silently crept from the room. Left alone, the formidable mountain chief sat on the floor, placed the baby in his lap and wept bitterly.

Chapter 2

Prophecy

Kshayarsha stood behind the king's chair fidgeting impatiently. The elders, as always, were discussing something of great importance, but for some reason, the prince had no desire to listen to their argument today more than ever. Some strange longing beckoned him to the open meadows outside with undeniable force. The prince blamed his unusual mood on the upcoming wedding he'd been wrapped up in.

What a lucky star Bagha was born on. He lives no worse off than me, and in return, no one's forcing him to marry an old spinster! The prince envied the boy roaming about freely outside.

He knew his father well; the Great Darayawahush would never break the law. When the time came, the camp of Ten Thousand Immortals would kneel and offer their prayers to Ahura-Mazda and finally be allowed to rest. The exhausted warriors would settle down around their bon-fires and drift into well deserved slumber.

Midnight was slowly approaching yet the crotchety elders hadn't even rightly started their debate. Strained silence settled into the king's roughly set tent.

It was here, amongst the Ten Thousand Immortals, that the sovereign's sons were trained; it was here, that future kings and generals were crafted. One torch, fastened to the central post and a copper lamp hanging from a chain above the table lit the room. One end of the tent was sectioned off by a pomegranate embroidered drape, behind which the king's bed was set. The sovereign's Parthian bow and Egyptian double edged sword were lain on a chest at the foot of the bed, while his Anshanian spear was stuck in the ground so that the gold lion head wouldn't be damaged. The rest of the space on the other side of the drape was almost entirely taken by the Ionian map covered table, around which eight people sat.

Kshayarsha had known each of them from his childhood. The oldest among them, the nearly seventy year old Satrap of Elam, the worthy Gauparuva, was the father of one of the prince's closest friend, Mardunaya. He always took his place at the king's right hand. The elderly man was known for his austerity and even now he glared so menacingly at the three men in front of him as if he doubted their words before they even said them. This stern browed, weathered noble, despite his respectable age, served as the King's Lance Carrier, the arshtibara and by strength and influence, only the red headed Utana, who sat at the king's left, could compare. This was exactly the same Utana who's daughter Kshayarsha would be taking as his wife.

If my bride looks anything like her father, I'm done for, and that's that. The youth tore his frightened gaze from his unsightly father-in-law to be and began secretly observing the noble beside him. Next to Utana sat the renounced Satrap of Media, Vidarna, clad in a shiny brocade robe. Among the king's companions, he was the most pleasant looking and if anybody were to ask Kshayarsha's opinion, upon being forced to marry a woman without seeing her first, he would much rather have Vidarna's daughter, than Utana's hideous spinster. But unfortunately it seemed that the elders were not at all interested in Kshayarsha's opinion in this matter.

The prince scanned the Median satrap's faultlessly chiseled face once more. Vidarna was only about sixty, but despite his relatively "modest" age, he had taken part in every one of Darayawahush's battles and was considered one of the most experienced supreme commanders in all of Persia. However, there was another elderly noble in the tent, Abar-Nahara's formidable satrap, Baghabagsha, who's strict appraisal the young courtiers feared above all. He had taken his respectable place beside the satrap of Elam. Kshayarsha turned his head that way. This grumpy, average height old man, covered with scars, was truly Bagha's grandfather, but the youngsters had never had the opportunity to speak with him. On the other hand, Bagha's father, the red cheeked Zopyrush, who sat across from the satrap of Elam, was the prince's mentor and had invested a lot of time in the young men's training.

Among his father's friends Zopyrush was the only one who Kshayarsha sincerely loved. He was far younger than all the others, about forty-five to forty-seven years old, but he still managed to put a lion's share into the suppression of Babylon's uprising at the beginning of Darayawahush's reign. For this, the sovereign especially valued him. Zopyrush was the only chubby noble at the Persian court and, as it seemed, had not yet finished blowing up. Khayarsha looked over the Garnet tunic stretched over his robust belly with a hidden smile. If not for golden brocade belt tightly wrapped around him, the noble's embroidered garment would fall open before everyone's eyes. Zopyrush perfectly combined his title of the man with the biggest appetite with being the cleverest. This was why the youth called him an old fox behind his back. At a single glance, the red cheeked, average height, chubby, middle aged man, left a kind and harmless impression, but everyone at the Persian court knew: Darayawahush's friend and personal advisor, set apart by his exceptional shrewdness and cunning, was one of the most influential and dangerous people in the Empire.

Beside Bagha's chubby father, sat Khayarsha's uncle, Darayawahush's youngest brother, Irdabanush. This straight featured, weathered man, with the sovereign's hazel eyes, was only forty, but thanks to his solemn and balanced nature, he had rightfully earned the position of a wise advisor at court.

The last member of this council, prince Irdabrdna, was Darayawahush's eldest son. From his mother's side, the prince's grandfather was the satrap of Elam, Gauparuva. Despite all of these advantages, this brown eyed, sparse bearded, big foreheaded half-brother of Kshayarsha left only pity in the heart of his younger brother, standing beside the king, in place of rivalry. Even now, instead of showing his worth to the elders, Irdabrdna was doing everything to remain invisible.

If one would have asked Khayarsha what these eight men had in common appearance-wise, he would certainly have said their beards. Thick beards, arranged in layered curls, reaching down to the chest were the pride of every Persian man. Kshayarsha himself impatiently yearned for his own newly sprouted, soft beard to grow to its full glory.

The four nobles sitting to the left and right of the sovereign were invited to the tent just to listen. Telling the news in detail was up to the three younger courtiers sitting on the other side of the table. Wrapped in a long Median fur robe, Darayawahush leaned against the high back of his chair, waiting patiently for the answer. There was no crown on the king's gray hair. In his circle of friends, he never weighed himself down with this precious adornment. From the royal objects, he only had the golden scepter, and even this he used as a simple pointer stick for the map. From time to time, the sovereign's narrowed eyes would shift from his younger brother, to his eldest son, and flicker over to his own loyal friend. Zopyrush, The King's Eyes in Babylon, already had the answer at the tip of his tongue, but the experienced courtier knew that to respond before the sovereign's own kin, Irdabanush, would be a grave mistake. The general impatiently dabbed at his chubby face with his sleeve and fixed his questioning eyes upon the young man as well. Irdabanush didn't rush his reply.

The question everyone eagerly awaited the answer to regarded the western satrapies and Ionian cities. Two years earlier in the city of Sardis, Athenian envoys had visited the king's older brother, the satrap of Lydia, Irdapirna, and had asked for protection from unfriendly Greek neighbors in turn for "earth and water". The fact that by giving this Attica was admitting a vassal dependence to the Great King of Kings probably evaded the emissaries. Of course, then Persia had gladly accepted the proposal.

After that, two summers had passed and the situation at the Empire's western boarders had changed entirely. Now their spies were already bringing alarming news from the Greek colonies and still free Hellenic settlements in Europe to the capitals.

It wasn't a coincidence that the king called together a secret council at the camp. Darayawahush fully trusted no one, and in the palace, even the walls had ears. The Great King wouldn't like to draw too much attention to the West Coast, but on the other hand, he couldn't leave the restless boarders without attention either. The wise king sensed that trouble was beginning to arise in the Aegean Sea.

It was not unusual for the sixteen year old Kshayarsha to be present at the secret councils. From the age of twelve, he had been following his father everywhere, but after reaching fifteen, at which time he was awarded the golden belt, symbolizing his adulthood, forever standing behind the throne became his honorable duty.

Kshayarsha already had opinions on many crucial matters, but he never took part in the discussions. Even the princes were allowed to speak only with the king's invitation. But when Darayawahush the Great would let his young son take part in national matters, was only known to him.

When the sovereign realize that his cautious brother would not give a straight-forward answer, he rephrased the question.

"Still, who are these Athenians? And what's going on, even amongst the Yaunas on our own land?"

For a long time Irdabanush had served as the King's Eyes in Lydia so he knew everything about his older brother, Irdapirna's surroundings. Ever since he came to the capital cities, the duty of spying on the foreign guests, as well as guarding the royal family fell upon him.

It was impossible to delay the answer any longer.

"O, Great Sunki," Irdabanush rose to his feet, "you know the whole western part of Asia has long belonged to us thanks to Ahura-Mazda. Even on Europe, across the sea, we have a strong hold. Most of the islands either pay tribute or already belong to us. Although, it is true that some islands still resist, Naxos and Delos, for example," the king's brother knelt over the map on the table and traced the places with his ringed finger, "but it's all a matter of time."

Kshayarsha stared with curiosity at the map on the table from over his father's shoulder, which wasn't hard, thanks to the boy's unusual height. All the rest, apart from Prince Irdabrdna, also started studying the brightly painted ox skin map with much interest.

"How much trust can one put in these paintings?" Baghabagsha asked doubtfully.

"This map was drawn by Hecataeos of Miletos. No one's better than him at this," Zopyrush replied to his father.

"I don't know..." The elderly man still shook his head uncertainly.

"The fact that those islanders have been looking across the sea is no news, we've known that for some time," Gauparuva grumbled.

Irdabanush glared discontentedly at the satrap of Elam from under his brows, but didn't dare say anything. The member of the renowned seven nobles of Persia could interrupt even the king, himself, this was why the young man swallowed his anger and continued his speech.

"Our brother, the noble Irdapirna informs us, that the islanders are frequently asking for our help themselves. Their nobles, if we can even call them that," Irdabanush smiled wryly, "wouldn't last two months on their little thrones without us. Yaunas, my dear Lord, are an unorganized and disobedient people. They don't honor their own government, never mind anyone else's. They live in the moment. They worship many gods, and like them, lead meaningless and shallow lives."

"A lot of people have many gods. We never interfere with the beliefs of our vassals. I don't quite follow where you are taking this discussion, Irdabanush," Utana noted calmly.

"What I want to say, worthy, Utana, is that there is no power in Hellas which can unify those brainless people. If the Great King wills it, we can easily conquer these Yaunas one by one. But we must also consider that controlling numerous islands and the European coast will be difficult even for us. It is not one country, Great Darayawahush," the young general turned once more to his brother. "They do not even have one king with whom you can make peace after conquering it."

Kshayarsha swept his gaze over the little islands scattered across the blue painted sea. He knew many of them by name. He even remembered what riches could be found on each. The islands that already belonged to or paid tribute to the Empire were marked with golden lion-headed pins. A few of the islands, rich with silver mines, still didn't belong to the Empire, but for some reason Irdabanush was not drawing attention to them. This surprised Kshayarsha. Then the biggest peninsula caught his attention: "Pelloponnisos". Not counting Argos, which he had heard about somewhere, the prince knew nothing about these lands.

"As far as I know, such an odd thing is only happening in Athens. If not kings, the islanders at least have tyrants," Gauparuva scratched his beard.

Kshayarsha immediately shifted his eyes over to the peninsula of Attica. Suddenly something splattered as a large blotch on the map. Everyone looked up. Oil was slowly seeping from the blazing copper lamp. Darayawahush's eyes froze for a second.

Someone's going to get a flogging tonight, Kshayarsha thought.

To bring the elders' attention back to the matter, the king's brother gave a quite cough.

"You speak the truth, my Lord Gauparuva. Among the Greeks, Athenians are the worst. They keep rambling on about this repulsive idea of people governing people!"

"What one doesn't hear at this old age!" Vidarna, who was the youngest among the old men, and even dyed his beard to appear younger, shook his head, sourly.

"The Aegean Sea is a bee hive, Great Darayawahush. In my opinion, to start any serious affairs with the Greeks would be a great mistake." The king's brother bowed respectfully and resumed his seat.

The words of his young uncle had a great impact on Kshayarsha.

How can a country exist without a king? The astounded prince reasoned to himself.

The king sat, thinking deeply for awhile, and then wordlessly shifted his gaze to Zopyrush.

"Great Sunki, you well know how much respect I put in honorable Irdabanush's wise words!"

At hearing this Kshayarsha smiled to himself. He knew the old fox's tricks like the back of his own hand. When the first words out of his mouth were compliments, the last, no doubt were insults. The only exception to this was the king himself. For Darayawahush, Zopyrush could only offer praise. Even if waken suddenly in the middle of the night, his startled cry would probably be "Hail Darayawahush!" From the lips of this man, never had a word of censure escaped. This degree of loyalty deserved even the Great Darayawahush's trust, and the king trusted almost no one.

"Honorable Irdabanush's words, of course, we never dare to doubt. They clearly reveal his deep knowledge and incomparable wisdom." With devilish sparks in his small, lively eyes, the noble praised the king's brother with a flattering smile and immediately went on to obliterate his advice. "Among the Yaunas there is much chaos, that's true, but isn't that in our favor? How many divided and disorderly nations have we already conquered? Have you yourself not traveled through their lands during the Scythian battles? You have already conquered many of their tribes. You and my father, the noble Baghabaksha, have even reached the 'Yaunas with sun hats.'"

At these words, Zopyrush shot a quick glance to the satrap of Abar-Nahara. *God forbid the old man count the mention of this campaign as my way of flattery.* Thankfully his father sat peacefully in his place, listening attentively to his son's argument. The words of the red-cheeked noble irritated someone else entirely.

"Fighting on land and fighting on islands or on the narrow sea shores aren't the same thing, Zopyrush!" Irdabanush broke in impatiently. "We can't even use our chariots properly over there!"

"But we can't leave the Yaunas unattended!" Zopyrush's temper flared. "They bring chaos to our lands! I've learned from a Babylonian Jew that

Ephesos and Miletos are always looking beyond the sea. We are not getting better news from Byzantion either."

The cities which Zopyrush had named and the lands attached to them covered almost half of the Empire's western coast.

How can this be true? The astounded Kshayarsha mused.

As if guessing his thought the elderly Gauparuva narrowed his eyes with suspicion:

"Isn't your fear a bit exaggerated, Zopirush?"

"I don't think I am exaggerating anything, worthy Satrap. Irdabanush spoke the truth, the Athenians are the worst. They came up with this idea of democracy! Never mind others, they don't give their own nobles peace. Persia is full of their runaway rulers. Even as we speak, their rabid ideas are poisoning our Greek cities. The islanders truly do look like a bee hive and bees are known to attack and sting dreadfully!"

"No, not unless you provoke them first, Zopyrush!" Irdabanush shot back.

Darayawahush's son, Irdabrdna had been sitting silently beside his uncle the whole time, obviously not eager to partake in the discussion. The sovereign gazed carefully at his eldest offspring, given to him by a Satrap's daughter. The King of Kings didn't like the prince's dormant character.

Kshayarsha knew beforehand that this secret council would probably yield no results. His father wouldn't even state his own opinion. King Darayawahush was looking at his oldest son with narrowed eyes and appeared to be deep in thought.

Suddenly at the tents entrance a young boy's messy head popped in and immediately disappeared. Kshayarsha shot a pleading glance over at his father. The king nodded his dismissal. The gleeful boy swiftly scuffled out. The guard bowed respectfully to the prince as he emerged from the tent.

The youngster was well respected among the warriors as well as in the palace. At the camp he was liked because of his amazing strength and bravery, and the palace was charmed by his even more amazing beauty. Kshayarsha's appearance could be summed up in one word: incomparable. The boy had already outgrown many of the best warriors, yet his red, childishly plump lips exposed his true age. Kshayarsha always dressed flawlessly. Today he clothed his long legs with silk garnet-colored wide pants, golden fish-scaled chainmail covered the Punjabian linen draping his wide shoulders, and on his feet he wore shoes brought especially for him from the Egyptian town, Anthylla. His soft, shoulder length raven curls were tied at the nape of his neck with a golden purl, and on his forehead sat a prince's crown. Refined in every aspect, he may have even left a soft impression, but from his beautiful almond shaped, almost black eyes, set against his bronze skin, emanated such a fierce predator-like essence that even many of the stern generals felt strange shivers in the presence of this boy.

My son has such a spirit within him; no one can deny him the throne! Queen Hutaosha had concluded with a pleased smile long before.

The noblemen half jokingly called this slim, curly haired boy Little Sunki – Little King, which made the other princes resent him deeply.

The beautiful Hutaosha, Kourosh the Great's oldest daughter, was not the king's favorite wife. Darayawahush' heart was conquered by the lovely Irtashduna, the queen's youngest sister, but among the king's wives, Hutaosha was the wisest and the most cunning. The cold and reserved queen didn't engulf Kshayarsha in motherly love; instead she gave him an enviable education.

The sixteen year old prince fluently spoke Arian, Aramaic, Babylonian and Elamite. Surrounded by Hellen slaves and healers, the boy took to Greek as well. The prince learned stars and ground measurements from Chaldean wise men. Hutaosha paid particular attention to her son's religious upbringing. Under his mother's guidance, Kshayarsha became a most sincere follower of the Arians' beloved prophet Zarathustra.

Even though Kshayarsha wasn't the firstborn of Darayawahush, thanks to his personal qualities and the blood of Kourosh the Great from his mother's side, among the princes he was undoubtedly the best candidate to become the heir to the throne.

The immortals' camp was set at the foot of the Zagor mountain range, because of which the heat broke off sooner there, making the nights pleasantly cool.

Emerging from the stuffy tent, the prince greedily breathed in the fresh Medean air and looked around. Bagha was nowhere in sight.

"Where has this useless pike disappeared to in the blink of an eye?" Khsayarsha quietly swore to his friend and called to a nearby immortal: "Datia, have you seen Bagha?"

"He was just here a moment ago." The warrior stopped sharpening his saber and headed for the young man. "Hold on, I'll find him right away."

"No, I'll find him myself."

Although it was late at night, the fires scattered about the field allowed the prince to see clearly. No one was sleeping in the camp; they were all scurrying about busily. Beneath the copper pots sitting atop dried brick, embers crackled cheerfully. Most of the warriors had already finished their suppers, although some were still eating heartily. Some were laughing, some arguing, in some places singing could be heard. Others were dancing and playing around. There were even those who managed to get some alone time behind some bushes with the jahikas, who permanently lived in the camps. The most prudent ones sat about fixing their armor and sorting their things. In short, everyone entertained themselves in whatever way they could.

When the smell of meat roasting on the spit was too much for the prince, walking between the fires, the boy felt his stomach burn. His supper would probably have been set by then, but Kshayarsha decided to look for Baghabagsha rather than go eat. Asking around, he finally ran into him by the blacksmith's. Crouched beside the immortals, stretched across the trampled grass, the young boy was arguing loudly with a man three times his size.

"I'm telling you, there's nothing to it!" The boy was waving his silver belt, broken at the buckle, in front of the man's soot-covered face.

"That may be so, but it is not my job. Go bring it to the goldsmith."

"I'm telling you to fix it!" Zopyrush's son moved threateningly toward the smith.

At seeing this, the prince sternly called to his arrogant friend.

"Bagha!"

Hearing the familiar voice, the lad immediately sprang to his feet and darted toward Kshayarsha.

"So, they let you out, my Prince?" he said, bowing with mock respect.

One would never believe, when looking at this skinny, disheveled and always joking boy that he was the only heir of the clever, plump Zopyrush, nor especially the ever frowning grandfather after whom he was named. Zopyrush didn't approve of his son's frivolous character and gave strict instructions:

"Baghabaksha, yes, the prince is your friend but keep in mind, one day he may become the ruler of all Persia. And a king deserves the highest respect. Never forget that!"

And now the mischievous boy fulfilled his father's orders in his own frivolous way.

"Bagha, come to your senses or I'll have your head!" Kshayarsha clapped his friend lightly on the shoulder but was unable to measure his own strength, and bore the boy to the ground.

The immortals lying about around them broke into a fit of laughter at the scene.

"What are you laughing at? You'd better get on with your own work!" Zopyrush's son sprang to his feet again and growled menacingly at the cheerful immortals.

"Will you look at that! He had a walloping and he's still at it!" The lanky boy's cockiness astonished the ox of a man.

"Are you surprised? The apple doesn't fall far from the tree," mumbled the immortal next to him.

"Instead of that useless talk, how about you roast us a couple of rabbits, I'm as hungry as a wolf! You're hungry too, right, Kshayarsha?"

"We're not your cooks, boy. But if the Prince wills it, we'd be happy to prepare his meal." One of the men laughed provokingly.

The prince shook his head no.

"What are you saying, Kshayarsha?" Bagha was appalled. "My stomach has all but shriveled up waiting for you, and you won't even order them to roast some rabbits?"

"Yeah, I can see that, glutton," the prince laughed and turned down the path leading to the outskirts of camp.

"Having a little here and there with the skauthi doesn't count as super!" Caught in a lie, the liar wiped his greasy mouth and ran after his long legged friend.

Zopyrush's empty-headed son was one quirky imp. Dressed in the finest clothes, due to his nobility, he still managed to always look a mess. Even now, the sleeve of his maroon brocade tunic was coming apart at the seams, half of it hanging already, and a huge grease stain soiled his bright green pants, but he couldn't care less. Pimply faced and bug-eyed, the youngster's tight curls were also forever standing on-end. Thankfully his beard hadn't grown in yet, for it too, would have probably been polluted with food remains and God knows what else. Bagha's caretakers selflessly fought his harmful habits with floggings and beatings, but there was no use battering a stone wall. He was completely hopeless.

Bagha was two years younger than Kshayarsha and had spent his entire life with the prince. The reason for this was quite simple: Zopyrush, the brother-in-law and loyal friend to Darayawahush, earned Queen Hutaosha's trust as well. This is why his son grew up in the palace. The prince had many other companions, but they were all the flesh and blood of Darayawahush, which meant certain rivalry in the future. For this reason the queen brought this joyful boy for her son. True, through the veins of Baghabaksha also ran the Achaemenid blood, his mother was Darayawahush's full sister, but they couldn't bring a nobody from the streets, could they? The king's proud wife only regarded the members of the seven noble families as their equals.

"Where are we going, Kshayarsha?"
"To the horses."

"I thought I wouldn't see you until prayer time. What are our elders doing?"

"They are debating, and will debate some more. Your father as usual, cannot rest. If only you could see how mad our uncle is!" the prince grinned wolfishly. "But he won't show it because of my father. He knows how much the king loves that old fox!"

The friends turned down another path leading to the stream.

It was a beautiful warm autumn night. The moon shone brightly, set against the dark, star studded sky. At a nearby bush, the nobles' horses grazed lazily, occasionally whinnying in undertones as if afraid to disturb the serene ambiance. A little distance away, within a wooden fence, hundreds of horses were housed for the immortals. This was why the smell of manure was so strong in this part of the camp. From time to time, the stifled snickering of the warriors could be heard. No one was asleep here either. The guards and stablemen were also waiting for the nightly prayer.

Kshayarsha found his horse and lovingly began to stroke his steed. The thankful four legged friend playfully snorted at his master.

"Let's go for a ride, Bagha. We still have time before midnight." The prince untied the beast and fluidly swung onto its back.

"On an empty stomach? It would be better if we filled our bellies first," Bagha scowled but did as his friend.

As soon as the youngsters silently crossed the brook and kicked their horses into a gallop, one of the warriors sitting by the fire stood and called with a jackal's cry to the hidden bodyguard on the other bank that the prince was headed in their direction. Kshayarsha was never left alone even amongst the loyal immortals.

After a while, the prince slowed his steed and let him move at his own pace. As if understanding the rider's desire the smart beast looked back and resumed walking with slower steps.

Kshayarsha was feeling strangely restless that night, so restless that, although he had been hungry since the day before, he had no desire for food.

What's wrong with me? This matter confused the boy himself.

The friends rode silently for a while. Far to the east, where the bright, star-studded sky enwrapped the earth in a lovers embrace, the highest peak of the mountains of Media, Alvand, stood like a sleeping black giant. The life-giving north wind was blowing in the direction of the camp, holding the bustling noise at bay, so that it barely disturbed the calm of the night. The horses carefully stepped through the tall, lush, but already bowing, late summer grass. There were low bushes here and there, but the fields at the foot of Alvand were mostly grazing lands. The dizzying scent of wild flowers stirred there in the early spring, but now the familiar, lazy smell of hay snuck even into the fields. The king's palace in the capital of Media was counting down its last days of summer. Darayawahush would wait for one more new moon to be half filled; meanwhile on the fifteenth day, dedicated to the god Attar, they would celebrate Kshayarsha's wedding, after which the king's court would leave Ecbatana and move to the capital of Elam, Susa, for the winter.

"They say Amisiri is a real beauty," Bagha broke the silence first.
"They're probably lying. How can Utana's daughter be good looking?"
"What are you talking about, Kshayarsha? If she were ugly, why would the king wed her to you?"
"Because my father and her father have some old scores to settle."
"Yeah, I've heard that too, but your father repaid Utana a long time ago."
"What are you rambling about, Bagha?"
"I'm not rambling. You remember the old tale of how our Elders snapped that so called Bardia's neck. Don't you?"
"Yeah. That's when the seven nobles of Persia arose. Your grandfather received Abar-Nahara as a reward. Vidarna became the satrap of Media. Utana gained strength in Lydia. And our Mardunaya's old man became the Lord of Elam, the heart of the Empire. Ardunamush would have gotten a Satrapy as a gift as well, had he not journeyed to the world of the deceased. Only Vindafrana was cheated by fate. That wretched man got himself killed by the King for no reason."
"Your father still benefited the most. He got the whole Empire."
"The seven chose father as King themselves!" Kshayarsha stiffened.
"The wicked say that Utana deserved the throne more. That is why your future father-in-law's family is the only one in the Empire who doesn't pay a tribute to the king. They say that this is how Darayawahush gave him his thanks."
"If you don't learn how to hold your tongue, it will undoubtedly be your doom, Bagha!"
"For what? I'm only saying that your father has already paid his debt to Utana. There is no need for you to marry his hideous and old spinster of a daughter," Bagha didn't withdraw.
At remembering his future wedding, Kshayarsha sighed heavily, cast his sad gaze over the moon-lit meadow, then looked to the sky and, in order to deprive Bagha of the opportunity to ramble on, began surveying the stars. Knowing how much his friend loved to gaze for hours at the celestial bodies, Zopyrush's son was forced to keep shut for a time.

Studying the writings of Chaldean wisemen always filled Kshayarsha's soul with uncommon pleasure. He knew "Enuma Anu Enlil" almost by heart. Bagha, of course, considered all of this entirely useless stupidity for a soldier and always slept soundly during lessons with the Chaldian wisemen. Even now, as if mocking him, the cerulean sky was filled with glittering stars. This meant that Kshayarsha would be lost to him for a good while. On the other hand, the prince himself looked rather pleased. The blissful fireflies seemed as if they were playing with the somber prince: they laughed, winking and hiding childishly and then appearing again on that vast stretch of darkness. Kshayarsha knew the stars' arrangements by heart. On a clear night he could easily find the ox, the lion and all other constellations, but tonight's sky was completely different. It looked more like a magical world of dancing fireflies. The boy could even have sworn that he could hear the distant song of the stars. This astonishing sight entertained Kshayarsha at first, then slowly reeled him in, and finally, invited him into its twinkling wonder world. The prince, enchanted by the stars, watched them play their strange games. Suddenly a new starlet appeared as a bright dot to the north, then as if ignited by a life-giving breath, it flickered and burst into a brilliant star.

"Look, Bagha, look!" the price burst out pointing up.

"Where, where?" His companion stared up at the sky with widened eyes.

"Over there, how can you miss it? In the sky, to the right!" The astounded boy was frantically waving his arms in the air.

Baghabaksha tried to focus his gaze to where the prince was pointing. Next to Kshayarsha's star another suddenly appeared, it flared with all its might and as if yanked from its place, streamed across the sky beyond the horizon.

"There, I see it!" the exited boy shouted. "What do you think this could mean? They say it means war is coming!"

"No, Bagha, you didn't see anything!"

"What do you mean I didn't see anything?" he was astonished.

"My star was just born, my friend!" the prince cried out wildly, filled with new happiness out of nowhere.

"You probably imagined it. How could you possibly have seen the birth of one tiny little star in the vast sky?" Baghabagsha doubted but at seeing Kshayarsha's angrily furrowed brows, rephrased his disbelief: "How do you know it's your star?"

"I know. I feel it in my heart," the prince smiled.

"What a great treasure! What use can a little light in the sky be to a man? It would be even better if you found us a tasty rabbit in the grass somewhere," the boy retorted coolly.

"How hopelessly stupid you are, pike. Something exceedingly important to me has taken place tonight, but why do I bother explaining it to you? Your feeble mind won't understand anyway."

"Right, it won't understand! I understand everything that is necessary and important perfectly." Bagha laughed cheerfully.

Chapter 3

Wedding

Amisiri leaned against the high back of an armchair, observing the beautiful view of the landscape through the narrow window. From where she sat she could clearly see the striking scene of an enormous mountain range, covered with thick forests and the glacial peak of Alvand, shimmering like diamonds as the sun reflected off its shiny surface. Utana's youngest daughter grew up in Lydia and had often spent the winter in Susa and Persepolis, but it was for the first time that she visited Ecbatana. Amisiri had heard much about the fascinating wealth of the capital of Media, but what lay stretched out before her surpassed all expectations.

The seven sided wall surrounding the city charmed her eyes with its golden figures dancing against the stone, glistening so brightly that they could be seen even from a distance. From above Ecbatana resembled some sort of paradise wrapped in autumn colors where many buildings, large and small, were scattered about like beautiful jewels. The glittering royal blue palace of the legendary Queen Semiramis was separated from Darayawahush's newly built colorful summer residence by fruitful gardens, from which was wafted such an aroma that even Amisiri, who wasn't known for a good appetite, wanted to drink a bit of nectar. The jug was sitting on the table right in front of her but the glorious lady was unused to serving herself.

"Uparmaya, pour me some wine."

The girl of about fourteen stepped from the meadow colored wall with white lilies and obediently filled her crystal glass. Amisiri quietly watched every movement of the maid, all the while thinking of the gossip she'd overheard:

Is it possible that this girl is really the sunki's illegitimate child? That would mean they have brought my own husband's half-sister as my personal maid. It does have the ring of truth to it. She has the sunki's squinting hazel eyes.

As soon as Amisiri tasted the water diluted nectar, she poured in out onto the floor.

"It's too warm. I want cold wine!"

There was no look of insult or annoyance in the servant's snaky, reticent eyes. The servant had already grown used to such behavior from the lady. The girl bowed her head modestly and silently slid from the room, carrying the jug away.

No, it must be a lie. If this bimbo were really the sunki's daughter, thanks to her baleful character she would reveal some kind of conceit by now.

At Uparmaya's departure, an elderly slave came into the room and briskly cleaned the mess off the floor, but Amisiri didn't even notice. She resumed observing the city through the window. Aiming to have a better look at the tower of the wall, she rose ever so slightly in her seat. Amisiri knew the tower had been erected by King Daiukku, the founder of Media, safeguarding Ecbatana from invaders.

Are all seven towers really covered with gold?

Utana's daughter had heard about the wealth of the kings of Media, and also of their aspiration for glory and magnificence, but she never imagined that so much gold could be spared for purely ornamental purposes.

Hmm. The king was clever; he might have foreseen that one day, here at these walls, the last crown prince of Media would meet the end of his miserable life. So he had it decorated suitably. The lady smiled maliciously.

The tale went that eighteen years ago, Frada, the son of Upadaranma, the last king of Media, announced himself to be king and renamed Kshastrita. The seven famous noblemen of Persia suppressed this uprising with the utmost severity. Without even a thought, Darayawahush put out the eyes of the usurper with his own hands, cut off his ears, nose and lips, pulled his tongue out at the seams and crucified him at the wall of Ecbatana. His fate of his allies was no better. Under his orders, all of the noblemen participating in the upraising were sought out and as punishment, skinned alive. Then he had their skins packed with hay and hung next to the impostor over the great wall.

It was not in the least bit painful for the Persian maiden to remember the cruel, bloody day. On the contrary, Amisiri was very proud that her father, Utana, participated in the repression of the revolts in the first years of Darayawahush's rule. She considered that the deeds of her glorious father would secure the future of his daughter. Although, even at first glance anyone would see that for such a beautiful woman, a place in the royal palace of Persia was ensured even without the aid of her parents.

Amisiri was of average height. She somewhat resembled a flawless statue with a face that shined a stunning, icy beauty. From her pale complexion sparkled wide dark eyes, full of such vigor that one would swear that the spirit of some ancient sovereign had inhabited her body. If only Amisiri knew how to smile, her ruby lips, and teeth that could be mistaken for pearls, would probably have given her an unfeigned womanly charm and delicacy. But Utana's daughter hardly ever smiled. Actually, she knew how, but her smile evoked not affection, but a strange sense of anxiety in the hearts of those who beheld it. Her long curly raven hair fell to the lady's knees, but even this truly feminine ornament couldn't soften her stately appearance.

Amisiri took great care of her beauty, but today was a special occasion on which Amisiri was to be garbed as a bride. Her majesty, Queen Hutaosha herself, directed the dressing ceremony. Amisiri was washed in a scented bath and dressed in a gold embroidered light blue dress. Over that they placed a long sleeved garnet brocade tunic. Her hair was polished with Arabic rose oils and plaited in the Anshan custom of eight braid. After that her chest and arms were decorated with adamant and ruby studded necklaces and bracelets. Her fingers were painted with colorful magical triangles, while her eyes and brows were painted black. And finally a refined golden diadem with dangling temple plates was placed on her head, a translucent gold philet was placed over her, and at last, the satisfied queen announced the beautifying of the bride complete. This long preparation left the physically feeble Amisiri so exhausted the she requested to be left alone in her room for a while. Now she was sitting in her armchair waiting for the noble ladies to return.

The snaky-eyed Uparmaya glided into the room with a new jug in her hands and poured cold wine into the lady's cup. Darayawahush's youngest daughter, Ardushnamuya and Amisiri's mother followed the servant in.

"Oh, heavens! There's no one more beautiful than my brother's bride! Am I right, auntie? Amisiri looks like a star plucked right from the sky," cooed the youngest daughter of Darayawahush, quite unable to withhold her admiration.

The princess was around ten or twelve years old. While she didn't shine with beauty like Amisiri, she was the most sincere one of the royal family, because of which, some considered her not as clever as the others. But fate hadn't punished her because of this. The most desirable young man in Persia, the king's nephew, Mardunaya, had set his eyes on her.

Darayawahush's older sister, Amisiri's mother considered her daughter as the most beautiful Lady in the Empire. She contentedly scanned the bride once more and unable to find a flaw, cried cheerfully:

"It's time Amisiri, the Prince is waiting for us!"

I don't care, he will wait! I had to wait for ten years! The bride thought spitefully, but didn't say a word aloud, wary of her cousin's innocent ears.

Amisiri saw Kshayarsha for the first time in Pasargadae Ten years ago. The six year old prince, along with his elder brothers had stood beside the throne of his father, receiving valuable presents sent from distant satrapies with royal dignity.

"Look, what a charming boy he is. He will become a striking young man one day and your Lord, Amisiri." The lady had whispered to her daughter.

The proud girl had intently watched the boy, standing next to Darayawahush, and saw nothing but a child covered with gold.

"Is this to be my husband?" Amisiri turned in indignation to her mother.

The king's sister looked around uneasily and pinched her daughter on the arm.

"Hush you fool, hush!"

That day, Amisiri was completely heartbroken. So many brave, handsome young men were there, but for some reason, fortune had presented her with this skinny little boy. Amisiri didn't intend to fall in love with this ornamented little puppet. Before, the future had seemed very desirable to her, for she wanted to be queen, but the image of this infant humiliated her. From that day she hated her little bridegroom from the bottom of her heart. Presented with many opportunities to meet her husband to be, Amisiri declined them all.

Time passed. Amisiri knew that today not an infant, but a tall, well-shaped, handsome young man would stand beside her. She glanced at the prince several times from the window, but the feelings of the proud maiden which had been strengthened over many years, couldn't change so easily.

Losing her appetite from the unpleasant thoughts, the bride glanced at the wine filled cup and headed to the exit. Both noble women followed the beauty.

The enormous verandah was already full of Persian and Median nobility, waiting for the ladies. Baghabaksha, hair greased and dressed in a bright lizard-green tunic, the attractive Marduniya, wrapped in a sable robe, and some other fancy young nobles were chatting cheerfully with Amisiri's brothers: Smirdamna, Anapa and Patirampa. All of the groom's eleven brothers were also nearby. Although all of the young men gathered were pleasing to the eye, none could compare with Kshayarsha, standing a head taller than the rest. And the reason for this was not only because of his unusual height and striking face. As though the advantages given to him by nature were not enough, his clothes also stood out. In a swarm of bright, cheerful colors, his silver attire, even in its monotonous shade, overpowered all the others. The sword and belt attached to his hip were also silver and the ankle-length white-lily embroidered tunic with adamant studded shoulders, the prince's crown upon his brow, and the pearls woven into his hair with hidden strings, also all gleamed silver. Today, as a future husband, he represented the moon and stood out from the other youths, as the moon among the stars. The groom was entirely ready to meet his sun-bride. The fact that he was spreading the scent of jasmine in a world of rose and poppy was also one of the ways that he demonstrated his aspiration of exceptionality. Engaged in a conversation with his friends, Kshayarsha glanced every now and then at the palace entrance.

This giant thinks that he deserves the best of everything from birth. Let's see how his proud spirit accepts having Utana's old daughter for a wife. Prince Ariabirna tore his venomous gaze from his older brother's adamant studded slippers and looked to the palace himself.

Kshayarsha and his envious younger brother were not the only ones who were using up the last of their patience. With his hands clasped tightly behind his back, Darayawahush, clad in a golden brocade robe had his head bowed under the weight of his crown, pacing impatiently across the terrace. Zopyrush was trying to keep pace with the king, but couldn't quite keep up. The nobleman was dapping at his moist face with the hem of his sleeve, while quietly whispering of some important business.

"They better not be late!" the king growled threateningly and looked up at the sky.

It was a beautiful day in Ecbatana. The warm autumn sun was already reaching zenith. The magians were beginning to worry.

Since Darayawahush had inherited the Persian throne, he had tried his best to strengthen the belief in Ahura-Mazda, at least at the Royal Palace if not the whole Empire. Among the gods worshiped by the people of Persia, the king had chosen this god as the protector of his royal family and the Empire. Up to this point in time, nobody at the Anshan palace had paid much attention to any spiritual ceremonies. But Darayawahush had changed everything. It was true that the king himself didn't know too much about religion, but his sharp mind easily acknowledged that well thought out sacred rituals would serve to extend his power.

According to the Anshanian decree, the wedding ceremony was to start before midday, yet for some reason, the women were tardy. Darayawahush was slowly losing his temper.

Finally, at the entrance of the palace, a group of noble ladies appeared, led by Queen Hutaosha. Amisiri followed the queen with her head bowed, and the ladies, with Queen Irtashduna trailed behind at a distance.

"Oh, it was worth the wait!" the sovereign glanced at Amisiri with admiration and motioned Utana to join him.

I think this woman might not be ugly after all. Kshayarsha's heart fluttered with hope at seeing his bride.

The prince tried to observe Amisiri beneath the phillet, but couldn't make anything out clearly.

"I'm handing you, my son, the worthy Utana's respectable daughter Amisiri." The sovereign's gruff voice broke him from his reverie. "From this moment you are her Lord and master. Let almighty Ahura-Mazda bless you and the generous Anahita grant you many children!" Darayawahush took the bride's hand and the two fathers escorted the maiden to her groom.

As instructed by the magians, Kshayarsha gently kissed the palms of his beautiful bride.

The owner of such delicate fingers truly cannot be ugly. The young man's sensitive lips enjoyed the touch of his bride's velvety skin.

Amisiri quietly took her place next to him. The main part of the ceremony was about to begin. The head magian of Ragae, Memucan, wrapped in a blue and green robe and white turban, separated himself from the attending people and lead the bride-groom to the blazing fire set atop a bronze alter in the center of the pink tile covered terrace of the apadana.

"Let us forfeit our sincere devotion to the merciful Attar and ask the son of the Almighty to purify the newly born family in his sacred flames."

Meanwhile the sun reached its pinnacle and the entire procession fell to their knees, sending a worshiping prayer to Ahura-Mazda. Unexpectedly the conversation Kshayarsha had with an old eunuch that morning while he was being dressed resurfaced in his mind.

"I thank Great Marduk that I, an unworthy slave, have lived to see your wedding day. I remember the day you were born like it was yesterday, our glorious Mar Biti," the old man's eyes watered at his overwhelming emotions. "I knew from the very beginning that you were different from all the others."

"You only thought that because you had to take care of me, Banija. Every caretaker loves their charge particularly." The prince, standing before a sliver glass, smiled down at the servant from over his shoulder.

"Not only because of that," the eunuch waved his hands no and wrapped a silver belt around his deified prince. "When you were born, the fifteenth day was dawning after the birth of the moon. Do you know what this omen meant?"

"Of course I know, Banija." Kshayarsha adjusted the belt and appraised himself in the mirror with satisfaction. "Every fifteenth day of the month is dedicated to Attar. So my element is holy fire."

"You are right, oh wise Mar Biti. But if you will allow, I'll share another secret with you."

"What secret?"

Baghabagsha, who had been lying about lazily on the pillows scattered across a rug up until now, perked up with interest.

"In Babylon we say that a man's life is like a full moon. It must be full. When you were born, a half moon was shining in the night."

"What are you rambling on about, you wicked old sorcerer?" Zopyrush's short tempered son growled at hearing this.

"What are you trying to say, Banija? Do you mean that I'll only have half a life?" Kshayarsha was also taken aback.

"What ..? May both our gods protect you from such an ill fate! That is not what I meant!" the old man defended. "The Chaldian wise men say that however much of the moon is missing on the night of a man's birth will be filled by his other half, as in his wife. If a man is born on a new moon, in order to keep nature's balance, the god's will grant him a much smarter and more beautiful wife. If he is born on a full moon, he will be given a stupid or ugly wife. If this is true, my handsome Mar Biti, then you will have a wife fully your match."

Kshayarsha was relieved and motioned to the maid servants frozen nearby to begin fixing his hair. The servants immediately grabbed the stools brought especially for this purpose and circling around the prince, climbed up, and began their task. Watching this, Zopyrush's son burst into laughter:

"What are you talking about, Banija? Where are we supposed to find a woman like Kshayarsha? Don't you see the size of this giant? And his head is bursting with so much useless knowledge," Bagha was snickering mockingly. "Besides, you forgot the main point: one fine day, Kshayarsha will become king, and like his father, have many wives. So instead of one brainy beauty, countless dim-witted pretty girls will fill the empty half of his moon."

"You're the one mistaken, my boy, not me. A man may take many wives, but there is only one other half for him."

The words of the elderly servant cheered Bagha even more, but for some reason, they stayed in Kshayarsha's mind.

"How am I supposed to recognize the one among all of these beautiful women, Banja?"

"Oh, you won't have to do that, Mar Biti. Your heart will know when you see her. What's most important is that you realize this in time, because it turns out that most people run through their whole lives so that, entertained by other unimportant matters, they never manage to recognize their other halves."

The prince fell into thought.

"How can you listen to Banija's mumbling, Kshayarsha? How does he know of these matters? If he were at least a man. He's a eunuch!" Bagha was indignant.

Although Zopyrush's frivolous son spoke the truth, the kind servant's words took root in Kshayarsha's mind so that, instead of listening to Memucan's heated prayers, he was listening to his own heart, thinking, *'God forbid I don't miss recognizing my other half.'* Not when the king was loudly blessing the young couple, nor during Memucan's long hymn did the prince feel anything special. Instead, when he caught sight of Bagha, who had sprung up beside the chief magian, his heart filled with anger.

Didn't I warn him to leave this honorable duty to Mardunaya? Kshayarsha grinded his teeth, but his quite outrage and occasional angry glances couldn't worry his arrogant friend less.

When the sacrifice to the holy fire began, Bagha, glowing with pride, first passed a bewitched wooden twig to Memucan. While this magical offering was crackling in the fire, spreading a pleasant scent, the curious boy began inspecting the next sacrifice. This time they were giving the fat of a sacred animal to Attar. Which animal had be chosen for this purpose, or how the melted fat was prepared was a Ragaean secret and not even Kshayarsha himself knew anything about it, but this didn't prevent Bagha from lifting the top of the jar, sticking his wide nose in it and taking a sniff. All of this enraged the groom so much that, never mind peeking at his wife or listening to his heart, he barely even managed to stand modestly in his place. When Memucan turned to Baghabagsha for the next sacrifice, caught red handed, the boy let the alabaster jar slip through his fingers. Thankfully, Mardunaya was standing right beside him. With a miracle, he managed to catch the precious container in his swift hands and immediately handed it over to the chief magian. All of this happened so quickly that most of the onlookers hadn't noticed a thing, although those who needed to see it saw everything. Steam rose from Zopyrush's ruddy cheeks.

"I'll skin that wretched boy alive!" grumbled the noble, puffed up even more from anger.

"Trust me, Zopyrush, when the time comes, your feather brained boy will turn into a brilliant general," Darayawahush smiled, "but still take nine layers off his back tonight. It'll help him wisen up."

As a third gift, Memucan fed Attar the most precious incense. With this the the fire worshiping was done and everyone moved to the gushing fountain in the palace garden. Walking down the wide stairs of the apadana and going through the sweet smelling walkway lined with apple-laden trees pleased Kshayarsha.

If it were spring, pinkish- white flowers would be scattered all over this place, the thought crossed the prince's mind, though he didn't know why. He couldn't manage to keep his attention on his wedding today, and this disappointed him greatly.

Zarathustra's followers always worshiped Apo, the element of water, after Attar.

Here Memucan offered two fresh cypress leaves and a bowl of milk to the holy spring of Apo. This time, they didn't let the restless Bagha anywhere near the magians. On behalf of the groom, Mardunaya served as Memucan's helper, but Kshayarsha was still strangely alert and instead of plunging entirely into the wedding secret, he felt more like an accidental witness, watching from the side.

Everything is that brainless Bagha's fault! This pike is messing up my mind too! the prince thought, but he was angrier at himself than at his young friend.

When the fire and water worshipping was over, the emotionally exhausted Kshayarsha felt relieved. After this the king and queens, the recently married couple and the whole suite of nobility moved back to the apadana of the palace.

The brightly lit hall, adorned with tall, vibrant columns, beautiful cloths and exotic plants, was a magnificent sight to behold. The wedding tables were overflowing with exquisite foods and rare delicacies. The place was full of guests. The festively dressed guards were standing along the walls. Covered with gold and silver, it was difficult to distinguish the immortals from the guests, though they didn't participate in the feast and were always ready to defend the royal family from any danger with their own lives.

Darayawahush approached the head of the table and together with his queens and the newly married couple took a seat. The young groom was a little tense. Before he completed all the necessary ceremonial rites he knew that all eyes would remain on him. Seeking some comfort, the prince took a quick peek at his friends, but Bagha, instead of offering a reassuring smile, stuck out his insolent tongue.

What else could I expect from this fool? Kshayarsha sighed deeply and turned to Amisiri. He was supposed to see his wife's face for the first time today so he was noticeably worried.

Oh god, just don't let her have a long nose! He finally gathered his courage and pulled the veil from the lady's face.

Kshayarsha momentarily lost his voice from astonishment. He had seen many beautiful women, but he couldn't imagine that such perfection even existed. A barely noticeable haughty smile had snuck into the corners or Amisiri's mouth. Otherwise she appeared absolutely calm.

I probably imagined it.

To conceal his bewilderment, Kshayarsha quickly reached for a loaf of bread, broke it and handed a half to his beautiful wife. Then the prince, slicing a piece of roast meat, tentatively placed it on their shared wedding platter. Kshayarsha bit off a piece and offered the rest to his wife. Amisiri wordlessly took the offering from her husband. Taking a sip of wine from the golden bowl, he let his wife drink the rest. Head bowed, the lady emptied it.

The old Anshan wedding ceremony of eating from a common dish was complete. The guests congratulated the young couple with joyful shouts and the feast began.

"What a beautiful bride, really worthy of a Sunki!" the people were murmuring amongst themselves.

Soon the guests were getting tipsy; the hall was filled with merry calls and laughter. Some drank, some ate, and others discussed business matters as always. The servants slipped among the guests silently and from time to time, a guard would carry away an absurdly drunk man or two.

Smiling quietly, Darayawahush surveyed the hall with his piercing eyes. The sovereign seemed satisfied. As soon as he got the chance, Kshayarsha furtively started studying his wife.

They told me the truth. She is like a flawless goddess, and doesn't even look old! the prince noted with satisfaction.

"Treat yourself, my Lady," Kshayarsha pushed a silver bowl of fruit to Amisiri.

"Thank you," she took a ripe pear without looking.

She's being timid. Kshayarsha smiled to himself.

"You must be tired; it has been a long day."

"Not so much, no," Amisiri replied curtly.

"My friends are sitting over there, where are yours?" the prince didn't want to give up.

"I don't have any," the same odd smile played across the maiden's lips.

Kshayarsha was surprised, but said nothing. He was even a little bit disappointed. He had imagined his own wedding much differently. The baffled prince's eyes wondered over to his friends. Zopyrush's son was arguing with the rest of his friends, his arms waving about.

I wonder what they're talking about. The young groom wished to be with them.

"Oh, what a delightful night is awaiting our prince," Bagha burped enviously.

"And how would you know?" Marduniya teased.

Among Kshayarsha's close companions, he was the eldest, almost nineteen. Tall, well built and broad shouldered, with straight features, hazel eyes, and a soft beard, the only son of the powerful Satrap Gauparuva, and more importantly, the most promising commander of the Persian army, he easily charmed the beauties at court, but Marduniya had paid no heed to the ladies. He was already engaged to Darayawahush's youngest daughter.

"Gauparuva's son only loves Ardushnamuya because she is the king's daughter," the bitter ladies gossiped. It was a lie though; Achaemenid from his mother's side and the only son of the powerful Gauparuva, his future was already guaranteed at the Persian court without the help of his future wife.

The harsh snap from his older friend made Baghabaksha flush in anger. The flustered boy ruffled up with discomfort.

"Yes, yes, I'm talking to you. What do you know?" the tipsy Vidarna Jr. went along with Marduniya's joke.

"I do know!" the boy replied with dignity, almost in tears.

The drunken young men neighed like horses and banged their fists on the table.

"Don't tell me you've already seen a woman," the Armenian Tigran stretched before the boy.

"Right, I have!"

"Where, in the bed of the old fox?" one of the youngsters exclaimed impudently.

"No, in the bed of Kshayarsha!" the offended boy jumped to his feet.

Mardunaya caught him by the arm and quickly made him sit back down.

"Hush up you fool!" he whispered. "Do you want to make the married couple quarrel on their wedding night?" Marduniya was already regretting having unwittingly started this senseless joke.

"Confess, Bagha, has Kshayarsha already introduced you to a woman, or are you just boasting?" The elder son of the satrap of Media narrowed his eyes.

"Why would I lie, Vidarna? You know the house in the Greek suburbs in Shushan, don't you? Well, you should know that the prince never goes there without me," boasted the boy.

The young men looked at each other, surprised. They were all well aware of the Greeks' house. It was called Greeks', but actually one could meet beautiful women of all races there. The question was how could the inexperienced Baghabaksha know that? The prince already had his own women. The fact that Kshayarsha quietly and shamelessly visited the noble ladies' beds as well wasn't news either. But visiting the city brothels was really something.

Astonishment soon turned to admiration. Quickly believing what they had heard, they clapped Baghabaksha on his back as a sign of approval. Thoroughly delighted by the praise of his older friends, Bagha almost jumped from his skin with joy. Only Marduniya seemed troubled by what he had just learned.

The prince, noticing his friends' laughter, was completely taken by jealousy.

"Look how happy they are," he turned to Amisiri.

"Sure they are. What else can they do but entertain themselves and have a bit of fun?"

The prince straightened up right away. His newlywed wife astonished him more and more.

"What about us, my Lady? How are we to amuse ourselves?"

"Power is our amusement," Amisiri cut him short.

Confused, Kshayarsha swallowed quietly.

When the prince finally entered his bride's bedchamber, it was well after midnight. At seeing Kshayarsha the noble women lounging in the room with Amisiri scurried out at once, and the eunuch closed the heavy doors behind them.

The room shone with splendor. A golden sun embroidered grass-colored carpet was sprawled across the ruby floor. Sky blue and white silk covered the walls adding to the magnificence of the bedchamber. On a low marble table, there stood a golden bowl of fruit, a rhyton studded with precious stones and a jug filled with Kolchian wine. Over the narrow window pane, colorful netting was drawn. The bed, elegantly decorated with myrtle flowers, stood in the middle of the room, warmly inviting the bridegroom. The servant girls had scattered red rose petals and ripe, bursting pomegranates around the room. The only torch, hanging on a wall at the farthest corner of the room, danced cheerfully with every breath of the playful breeze, adding a fairy tale mystery to the nest prepared for the sweethearts.

Here every detail had its hidden meaning and Kshayarsha knew how to read this secret language. The myrtle represented the maiden's purity. The pomegranate was for the groom's versatile love experience. The rose meant passion. The wine and fruit - fertility. As for the fire and wind, these were Kshayarsha's elements, himself.

He had already forgotten the unpleasant feeling that had been evoked at the wedding table. Tenderness burst its way into Kshayarsha's chest at the sight of his lovely wife. Young, but quite experienced in Anahita's worshipping affairs, the bridegroom was ready to engulf his wife in the fire of passion.

Kshayarsha approached the bed, drew the curtains aside and… was left incredulous. His wife dressed in splendid Median white silk, embroidered in red and gold, was sitting on the bed, poorly hiding her spite toward her husband.

Don't forget, Amisiri, he is your Lord now and you must fulfill all of his desires, her mother's voice buzzed in her head.

No, Amisiri didn't think to refuse her obligations to her husband. The main duty of a queen was to give the Achaemenid dynasty heirs. Without that, neither her kinship nor great beauty would help the lady achieve anything. But she couldn't forgive her young husband those endless lost years of virginity.

Remember, a beautiful woman's weapons are charm and tenderness, curbing even the fiercest of sovereigns into inoffensive puppies, continued her mother's voice.

No! Amisiri obstinately shook her head.

There were other means than love and endearment to get what one wanted. The prince possessed quite a number of concubines for entertainment. Utana's proud daughter didn't intend to degrade herself by joining them.

I can handle my towering, beardless young husband! A disgusted smile twisted the lips of the self confident woman.

Kshayarsha leaned in for a kiss but was confused when he met Amisiri's cold and mocking eyes. What was that? A new way to show a virgin's coyness? While the youth was considering this, the woman lay back on the bed and revealed her naked body. This confused the young groom even more. He had never met such a strange creature. The breathless young man plucked up his courage and endeavored to kiss his wife once more, but she turned her face away. Kshayarsha straightened abruptly. There was no doubt about it: Amisiri wasn't interested in the prince's affection for her even a bit. Kshayarsha's desire for her vanished without a trace. All he wanted now was to get out of this place.

Come, if you dare! His wife's shameless eyes seemed to be mocking him.

Kshayarsha was just as stubborn as the young lady, but as spoiled by the ladies' as he was, the prince was unused to such a welcome in bed. The stone faced Kshayarsha rushed from the room and left the place with quick steps.

He had never felt so insulted before this. Furious, the prince almost ran to his room, biting his lips and bitterly scolding his new spouse.

Meanwhile, Amisiri sat on the bed, smiling cruelly. Utana's proud daughter seemed satisfied with her revenge on the blameless young man.

Queen Hutaosha was quickly informed of the prince's hasty departure from Amisiri's chamber the very next day. Troubled, she wanted to speak with her son immediately, but Kshayarsha had managed to go hunting with his friends in time.

The prince's behavior baffled the young noblemen as well, but even the bold Baghabaksha didn't dare to openly ask him anything. Behind Kshayarsha's back the young men gossiped worse than women, digging up different versions in order to explain his strange actions and finally came to a conclusion:

"Yes, Amisiri is very beautiful, but look at her eyes…Oh, how they shine! She is not a woman, I say! Poor Kshayarsha doesn't want to admit it, but he cannot lay with her. You'll see, he will marry a new wife soon enough and everything will be all right," the young noblemen agreed wisely amongst themselves.

Ten days later the queen had tried to meet with the prince once more, but in vain. Kshayarsha didn't intend to discuss these matters with his mother. Hutaosha, now seriously disturbed, appealed to the king for help.

At first, Darayawahush was astonished by Kshayarsha's actions, and then thrown into a state of alarm. The prince's untimely fancy could seriously harm the Empire's interests. Darayawahush wasn't about to offend Utana over such foolishness, nor did he plan to leave Kshayarsha without a worthy heir. The angry father immediately summoned his wayward son.

"You know why the sunki needs a queen, don't you?" Darayawahush attacked, not even letting his son fully enter the room. "To provide heirs and strengthen the country!" the sovereign answered his own question.

"You can have a whole army of mistresses for your fun and entertainment! I have not yet announced the heir. Beware, Kshayarsha! If you dream of becoming the sunki, give up this foolishness! I will not even ask you why you dislike Utana's worthy daughter, but who could be a better wife than her to you? Now leave and behave like a man! First you give me a worthy heir and only then can we speak of Masishta!"

The will of the king was clear. The Empire demanded total submission from the prince. Kshayarsha was very proud, but not even his injured self-respect could force him to say no to becoming Masishta, the heir. What other choice did he have? Pale from anger, the young man swallowed the insult. The very same evening, he appeared in his wife's bedchamber unannounced and dismissed everyone with a fluid motion of his hand. After this, the young husband grabbed her hand, cautiously but steadily led Amisiri to the bed, lay her down and swiftly lifted her skirts. The dazed woman became one with her husband before she could even make a sound. Kshayarsha quickly fulfilled his obligations, politely bowed his head and left the room without a word.

Astonished and breathless with pain, Amisiri lay there silently for quite a while. Then coming to her senses, a smile of pure satisfaction ran across her face.

I have won the first battle, future Sunki! A self satisfied smile played across the lady's lips.

The strange couple soon realized that such relations were equally beneficial for both sides. Kshayarsha would visit his spouse from time to time. They even resumed short polite conversations. The young prince, cured of any romantic feelings toward women for quite a time, concluded bitterly that all those love songs, played on the tayra during the feast were only fairy tales meant to fool the naive and returned to the familiar turmoil of his previous joyful life without any regret.

Amisiri wasn't wasting time either. She entangled herself in the affairs at court, full of intrigue and underhanded hostility so eagerly that soon she learned all the dark secrets of the Palace. Thanks to her cleverness and cunning, she became the most influential lady in the Empire, after Queen Hutaosha. To the joy of the royal family, the prince's beautiful wife became pregnant and in nine months gave birth to a son named Darayawahush. Kshayarsha already had his first born from a concubine, but he couldn't become the heir, so they named him Irdabanush after the king's youngest brother. After the birth all foolish gossip around Amisiri stopped and the couple's odd relationship was temporarily forgotten in the palace.

Meanwhile the king felt that the now settled Kshayarsha was ready for state affairs. As soon as the time was right, the young prince was assigned an exceedingly serious duty. Darayawahush sent his son to Armina to control the Northern satrapies. The prince began fulfilling his father's orders with such eagerness that he soon earned the respect and approval of the sovereign and his experienced courtiers.

The goddess Anahita also favored the glorious prince of Persia. Amisiri gave Kshayarsha two more children, a son, Vishtaspa and a beautiful daughter, Umati.

Time passed quickly. Peace settled upon Northern Persia, but to the West, clouds were gathering in the sky over the Aegean.

Connect with Tsira Gelen

Visit my website: http://tsiragelen.com

Friend me on Facebook: https://www.facebook.com/TsiraGelen.Author

Email me: tsiragelen@gmail.com

Thank you for reading my book. If you enjoyed it, won't you please take a moment to leave me a review on the site where you bought it?

Thanks!

Tsira Gelen

www.ingramcontent.com/pod-product-compliance
Lightning Source LLC
Chambersburg PA
CBHW020546220526
45463CB00006B/2209